To Nancy,

Hope you enjoy this story of my family and the course.

Bill Armistead

(Michael Carroll)

(Michael Carroll)

THE ORCHARDS

One Hundred Years

William S. Armistead

Designed by Hans Teensma | impressinc.com

Principal photography by Michael Carroll

Edited by Chris Jerome

Printed by Puritan Press

ISBN: 978-1-7923-8550-6

(Michael Carroll)

This book is dedicated to the memory of Elisabeth Skinner.

Contents

IV. A CHANGE AND AN OPEN

V. PEOPLE

VI. FROM TREE TO GREEN

VII. LOOKING BACK, LOOKING AHEAD

(Michael Carroll)

Introduction

This is a story about The Orchards, a golf course in South Hadley, Massachusetts, that was built for my great-aunt, Elisabeth Skinner. While I've made it as historically accurate as possible, I've also added commentary throughout the book, including insights into my family—not to make this a memoir, but to add depth to the story. I hope the reader will accept and appreciate these occasional intrusions.

I was raised in the suburbs of New York. My mother was Peggy Skinner, daughter of William Skinner, and she grew up at a grand estate in Holyoke, Massachusetts, called Dogwood. Every year my family drove up to visit my grandfather, who still lived in that exquisite home. We usually came up at Thanksgiving or Christmas, and unlike some other family trips, this was a visit we anticipated with glee.

My grandfather was loving and generous, his property was glorious, and the game room in the basement was the best in the country, or so it seemed to us. We would then travel to South Hadley to see Elisabeth, or Aunt Polly, as we called her. She was kind, modest, caring, and inquisitive, and her home was as magnificent as Dogwood, with beautiful rooms to wander through and 40 acres to play on (although her game room didn't compare).

I didn't play golf when I was growing up; tennis and baseball were more important to me. I started playing in college, though not very well. I was vaguely aware of The Orchards, the golf course across the street from Aunt Polly's home, but we never talked about it, or of golf at all, since no one in my immediate family played. Aunt Polly didn't mention it either. Only later did I learn of her prodigious golfing achievements, and that the course was designed by the legendary Donald Ross.

It wasn't until 1990, when I was 37, that I finally played The Orchards. That was my introduction to Bob Bontempo, the Club's professional from 1970 to 1995, who joined me for a few holes. I remember him congratulating me on my shots, though there wasn't much about my game to commend. He couldn't have been nicer or more accommodating. I thought it was because I was related to Elisabeth Skinner, and to a degree, it probably was. After visiting The Orchards a few times, I realized that Bob treated everyone that way. He was pleasant and inviting, and that reflected the Club's personality. It was friendly, relaxed, and unpretentious. So I joined The Orchards, even though I lived 300 miles away. The drive to Silverwood Terrace was worth it to me. I liked the atmosphere, and I loved the course.

Through some good fortune, I received Aunt Polly's golf memorabilia after she had passed away. The Donald Ross blueprints, the contract to build the course, an untouched scorecard from 1922, and her hole-in-one ball from 1929 all came my way.

This book has allowed me to relive these memories, to tell the story of the course's creation, to revisit Ross's masterpiece, and to talk about my family. Writing it has been a joy.

I thank the Centennial Committee of the Club for giving me this opportunity.

—Bill Armistead
Washington, DC
December 2021

Part One

Building a Legacy

I

William Skinner

"The smartest horse jumps the ditch."

AMERICA HAS BEEN a nation of immigrants, and, sadly, of slaves. Those who came of their free will did so for opportunity, or to escape oppression. In 1845, at just 20 years of age, William Skinner came to America, alone, for both reasons. His family lived in squalor in East London. His father worked in a silk dye house and his mother wove silk at home, but they made little money. William hoped to apply his extraordinary talent and energy to create his own business, something that was almost impossible in the class system of England. So he jumped at the opportunity to work at a dye house in America.

Textiles were among the first businesses to capitalize on the Industrial Revolution. Machines were developed to capture the power of moving water for looms and reeling. Americans were willing to buy domestically made silk if it matched the quality of European material, but the country lacked the skilled artisans who plied their trade in France and England. William sailed to America to fill this void and, he hoped, be rewarded for his efforts.

A packet ship took him to New York, and then horse-drawn coaches delivered him to Northampton, Massachusetts, where he went to work dyeing silk for Edward Vallentine. Seven years later, he went into business with Joseph Warner to manufacture silk, but the partnership quickly soured. Skinner was aggressive in his business dealings, while Warner was cautious.

In 1854, Skinner decided to set out on his own, and he built a silk factory along the Mill River near Haydenville, soon to be known as Skinnerville. He made silk twists and threads

This packet ship, painted by Edward Moran, is very similar to the *Toronto*, on which Skinner sailed to New York in 1845.

that went into garments. The business became incredibly successful. By 1873 he was employing 70 people and producing nearly half a million dollars' worth of silk each year.

William may have thought about expanding his facility someday, as his brick building was becoming cramped for space. If he wanted a larger factory, he would need a more consistent supply of water than the Mill River provided. (At times the water level was so low he had to close his operation until rain replenished the reservoir.) But those musings likely weren't on his mind on the night of May 15, 1874. It was threatening rain when he fell asleep, which was good. Having an adequate water supply wouldn't be an issue for the foreseeable future.

Shortly after 8:00 a.m. the next day, a local farmer named Collins Graves came racing into the hamlet from upriver. The dam in Williamsburg had burst! People had only minutes to save themselves, he yelled. Delia Stearns, one of Skinner's employees, rang the large bell, alerting the village of imminent danger. William was yelling for everyone to flee. "To the hills!" he shouted, which meant to the railroad embankment on one side of the river or above the homes on the other side.

Within 15 minutes his mill had been flattened by a 10-foot wall of water. Four people in Skinnerville died, but the other towns along the river had more catastrophic outcomes. Sixty people perished in Williamsburg, 50 in Leeds, and 25 in Haydenville. William's financial losses were estimated at $200,000, about $35 million today. When asked to comment on his bad fortune, Skinner gathered his family around him and pointed to a man who had lost his wife and children. "In comparison," he said, "I have lost nothing, and have reason to be glad it is no worse."

It wasn't long before leaders of nearby cities made William attractive offers to relocate his business to their sites. Holyoke, one of the contenders, was a newly created city on the Connecticut River, with canals extensive enough to accommodate many large mills. These waterways would ensure a safe, steady supply of water to power his equipment. To entice him to relocate to the city, the Holyoke Water Power Company offered William five years' free rent on a piece of land for his factory and a low-interest-rate loan to finance its construction. Plus, the company would give him a sizable plot on which to build a home. William said yes.

Within a year his business was in operation in the bustling city. With sons Will and Joseph at his side, he expanded the company's product line, weaving silk for linings and gowns, and eventually, satin for wedding dresses. The Skinner name became synonymous with the finest quality silk in the nation.

William summarized his feelings about the enterprise system in America when he said, "In this glorious country, we all stand equal in the race for success. . . . The smartest horse jumps the ditch." Shortly before he died, in 1902, William Skinner & Sons employed nearly 1,000 men, women, and children. Within a couple of decades, that number would grow to 2,000, making it the largest silk mill under one roof in the world.

"Make good in the world."—*William Skinner*

Top: A woman weaving silk at home and a soup kitchen in Spitalfields, 19th century. ***(Bridgeman Art)***
Above: William Skinner's mill in Skinnerville. ***(WGBY)***

Left: The mill in Skinnerville was destroyed by the flood, but Skinner's home survived. *(Sarah Kilborne)* **It was disassembled and shipped to Holyoke, where it was rebuilt. Members of the Skinner family lived there until 1959, when it was donated to the city of Holyoke. It is now Wistariahurst Museum, below.** *(Wistariahurst Museum)* **Opposite, top: The Holyoke mills of William Skinner & Sons in 1912.** *(Holyoke Public Library)*

Skinner helped establish a number of civic institutions in the newly formed city of Holyoke. Upper left: He was an early benefactor of the Holyoke Hospital, serving as its board president for many years. Upper right: Along with J. P. Morgan and two others, he provided the funds to build the new Public Library, which opened in 1902. Right: The Holyoke YMCA, where volleyball was first played, was another recipient of his financial support.

Mount Holyoke

2

Joseph Skinner

"Father liked to build things." —Elisabeth Skinner

JOSEPH SKINNER was 11 years old when the dam above the Mill River in Williamsburg, Massachusetts, collapsed. His family managed to escape the devastation, but not everyone along the river was so lucky. One hundred thirty-nine people died on May 16, 1874.

After attending high school in Holyoke, Joseph went to Yale University, graduating in 1883. Six years later, he and his older brother, William, were running the family's silk company. Will was in charge of marketing and sales, and Joseph oversaw manufacturing. It was a perfect fit. Joseph was the practical, conscientious one, with a solid engineering background, while Will was a playboy who enjoyed mingling with the elite.

In 1887, Joseph married Martha Hubbard of Danbury, Connecticut. They started a family in Holyoke, raising four children in a large and comfortable house not far from Wistariahurst, the home that was rebuilt from the ruins of Skinnerville. As the family grew, they yearned to get away from the noise and smell endemic to the growing industrial city, to a place where they could spend their summers.

In 1906 Joseph found a house on a 14-acre parcel of land in South Hadley, a town just across the Connecticut River, with small businesses, farms, attractive homes, and Mount Holyoke College. Earlier that year, he had replaced his father on the board of the College, so he was quite familiar with the town. The family enjoyed the summer months at their retreat, returning to the city only when school resumed. He bought additional acreage to raise chickens and dairy cattle.

It didn't take long for the Skinners to realize that South Hadley should be their year-round residence. Joseph decided to build a much larger house, one where he'd have space to entertain, with salons grand enough to display his growing

Joseph Skinner acquired the Summit House in 1908, then donated the former hotel and its 375 acres to the State of Massachusetts in 1940. ***(Painting by Phil Snyder, contributed by Clay Armistead)***

The back of the Skinner home in 1984. *(Richard Selig)* **The front entrance to the property from Woodbridge Street circa 1926.** *(Mount Holyoke College)*

Joseph Skinner (far right) at the 1924 Commencement with Ambassador Henry Morgenthau, Sr. *(Mount Holyoke College)*

Joseph and his brother, Will, donated the funds for Skinner Hall, which opened in 1916. *(Mike Riley)*

collection of period furniture and fine art. With the silk business in full stride, he could afford it.

When construction was completed, around 1915, the family moved to Woodbridge Street, across from Mount Holyoke College. They named their home The Orchards because of the many apple trees on the property. It would remain in the Skinner family for 72 years.

Joseph fell in love with the institution across the street. He shared his father's long-held view that women should get a college education, and he served on the Mount Holyoke board for 26 years, 20 as its president. He worked closely with President Mary Woolley to elevate the College's academic curriculum. He had "an unwillingness to be content with anything but the best," Emeritus Professor Nellie Neilson would say. And he showed an uncommon generosity.

William Skinner had told his children to "Make good in the world." As people of means, it was their duty to share their wealth. All the children took his words seriously, contributing large sums to many institutions in the area, including a settlement house for the company's female employees, and a chapel at the Second Congregational Church. One daughter, Belle, provided a substantial sum to rebuild Hattonchâtel, a town in France, after it was destroyed in World War I. The Skinners were wealthy, but they understood their responsibility to help institutions in need.

Joseph decided to share part of his fortune with the College. Along with Will, he provided the funds to build Skinner Hall, a building for recitations. He bought a house, The Sycamores, where college girls could live, and he helped finance the president's new home. To help attract scholars, he funded fellowships in art, history, physics, and chemistry. He made other contributions, often anonymously. Joseph was as engaged with the school as much as anyone could possibly be. He loved helping to plan its future and protect its well-being.

He also took great interest in the town of South Hadley. He acquired many old houses and renovated them—not to make a profit, but to bring them back to their original condition. Once restored, he would rent them for a nominal amount or sell them at an affordable price to community members. He purchased the Summit House, a historic hotel perched atop Mount Holyoke, five miles away, bringing electricity and plumbing to the building and paving the road so visitors could easily access the mountaintop. Eventually he donated the building and its 375 acres to the State of Massachusetts.

Throughout his life Joseph enjoyed building things or fixing up rundown properties, then contributing them to worthy causes. It was one of his ways of making good in the world.

Three of Joseph and Martha's children eventually married and moved out of their large home, but Elisabeth, their second child, never married. After graduating from Vassar she returned to the family estate. Her mother had rheumatoid arthritis, and Elisabeth helped the staff take care of her. The debilitating condition was slowly taking over Martha's life. Doctors tried to relieve her pain with gold injections, Joseph installed an elevator to bypass the stairs, and everyone provided comfort as best they could.

From an early age, Elisabeth was active, participating in a number of sports, including golf. She enjoyed it, and she was good. Approaching age 30, she was playing at Mt. Tom Golf Club in Holyoke, but that was a 20-minute car ride away. Not that Elisabeth cared; she seldom complained about anything. But Joseph wanted a more convenient place for her to play.

The Skinner estate. *(Bill Armistead)*

As a man of wealth who would do anything for his family, Joseph found the solution. There was a man, originally from Scotland, who had built four holes at Mt. Tom, where Joseph was a member. All he needed to do was acquire some land and have this Scot start building a course for Elisabeth.

So he contacted Donald Ross.

Freshman Handbook

of

Mount Holyoke College

Compliments of

The Christian Association

Bumming is not allowed. But if some day as you're waiting for the car to go in to town, a long low gray Rolls Royce draws up and the man who is driving asks you to ride in with him, you needn't think you're bumming if you accept because it's none other than Mr. Skinner, the President of the Trustees.

GOLF

Even though you are a beginner you will have an opportunity to play golf, for Mr. Skinner has opened his golf club to the members of the Outing Club. You can't help liking the course. The instructor will help you with your weak points.

Joseph in front of his Rolls-Royce. *(Mount Holyoke College)*

3

Donald Ross

"Golf has never failed me."

Donald Ross was born in 1872, in Dornoch, Scotland, a small town 200 miles north of Edinburgh hard by the North Sea. Here the wind can be strong and the rain substantial when storms blow from the northeast, conditions that brought misery to Ross in his job as golf professional at the local club. In addition to fashioning golf clubs and giving lessons, he was the course superintendent, so he had to mend the turf, repair the damaged bunkers, and groom the greens. He hated it. Getting down on his hands and knees was anything but enjoyable, but what he learned from digging in the dirt would serve him well in the years ahead.

Ross moved to America in 1899, lured by a job that would pay him triple what he made in Dornoch. He expected to be giving lessons and making clubs at Oakley Country Club in suburban Boston. But the course had only 11 holes, and the members wanted Ross to remodel them and add seven more to complete their layout. At age 27, this would be the first of hundreds of courses he would design in his career. The following year he established an office in Pinehurst, North Carolina. Ross would continue giving lessons at Oakley in the summers, but he wanted to design courses in southeastern North Carolina, where the soil for golf courses is ideal.

His reputation spread after the first two courses in Pinehurst were completed. In 1910, he was introduced to Lewis Wyckoff, a wealthy businessman from Holyoke, who was looking for someone to redesign Mt. Tom Golf Club, a course he played at home. Ross told Wyckoff he had to fulfill the two-year contract he had just signed as head golf professional at Essex County Club, but on completion he would travel to Holyoke. He arrived in 1914 and designed four holes at Mt. Tom.

Wyckoff was impressed with the young man, and they became good friends. As a promoter of golf in western Massachusetts, he understood how quickly America was embracing the sport. Wyckoff encouraged Ross to leave his professional duties at Oakley and spend his time exclusively designing golf courses. People had fallen in love with the game, and there was a huge opportunity for architects with Ross's skills. Only a handful of capable designers were working at the turn of the century. Charles B. Macdonald, A. W. Tillinghast, and Alistair MacKenzie were the best.

Donald Ross shortly after his arrival in the United States. *(Tufts Archives)*

They were building one or two golf courses apiece each year, but the demand was far greater. It is likely that Wyckoff offered to bootstrap the Scot, providing the necessary funds to expand his business. Whether or not he did, from that point on Ross's business grew dramatically.

It isn't clear that Ross visited South Hadley when the design for The Orchards' first nine holes was made. He had a heavy workload in Pinehurst and a crushing travel schedule. But there's enough evidence to believe he did, at least to make an initial assessment of the property. He lived in nearby Holyoke from 1915 to 1917 before returning to Pinehurst to live there year round. In 1921 he returned to Holyoke to complete the design at Mt. Tom, a project that would take two years to complete. With work about to commence at The Orchards, it's hard to imagine Ross would not have traveled 10 miles across the Connecticut River to be involved in its design, especially since it was a project for Joseph Skinner, a prominent businessman Wyckoff had introduced him to.

What is clear is that Walter Hatch, one of Ross's two design associates, brought a dozen men and a small team of horses to South Hadley from nearby Amherst in 1921. The Orchards would be a challenging course to build because most of the property consisted of wetlands; however, Ross and his team had tackled similar problems elsewhere.

Dornoch, Scotland, birthplace of Donald Ross. *(Alamy)*

Holyoke businessman Lewis Wyckoff *(Holyoke Public Library)* **and Mt. Tom Golf Club.**

Royal Dornoch Golf Club.

(Getty)

4
Building the First Nine Holes

"A sandy loam is by far the very best golfing soil." —*Donald Ross*

LOOKING DOWN the hill from what would become the first fairway, Walter Hatch saw some apple trees. The sight must have been beautiful. But farther down the slope was a swamp that extended from what is now the brook all the way to the 1st green. Ray Roberts, who lived at the edge of the property, didn't have to tell him about the mosquitos. They were everywhere. Much of the property Joseph acquired for the first nine holes was that way: wet, buggy, with no drainage.

There was a large pond, owned by Charlie Ford. One side was near today's 17th tee. The pond spanned the lower section of the 18th fairway all the way to Silver Street. Ford harvested the ice that formed there in the winter. Silverwood Terrace didn't exist, nor did any of the houses you see today on the street. Corn and potatoes grew in the area around the current practice range.

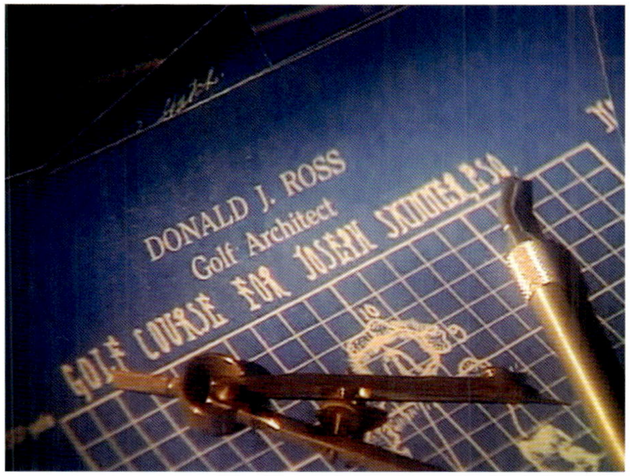

Walter Hatch drafted these blueprints in 1921.

Although tractors had been developed in World War I, they hadn't been employed for golf course construction in the early 1920s. Instead, horses pulling plows shaped the course. When working with sandy soil, Ross's team didn't do a lot of deep plowing, but this piece of land tended to clay, and to improve the drainage, it had to be pulverized with deep plows. This made for a slow, grueling process.

Hatch constructed brooks to help divert the water from the swampy land, and he drained Mr. Ford's pond. Customers would have to look elsewhere for ice in the winter. Then he focused on the greens, where the team usually did its best work. The contours of the putting surfaces had to be suitable for each hole, some with a steep back-to-front slope, others not. They measured only 4,000 square feet on average, which is much smaller than those that architects

Men and horses sculpting a bunker, here in Pine Needles, North Carolina. *(Tufts Archives)*

Building a fairway in Pine Needles. ***(Tufts Archives)***

build today. And they were durable. They had to be, to meet Ross's high standards.

It would take more than a year to complete the golf course, which measured a little over 3,200 yards from the first loop, and about 6,300 in total when the second loop was played, using different tees. When it was done, Joseph moved an old carriage house from his property across the street, which he modified into a clubhouse. On August 5, 1922, the course was open for play.

Ross associate Walter Hatch was the primary designer of the first nine holes.
(David Hosford)

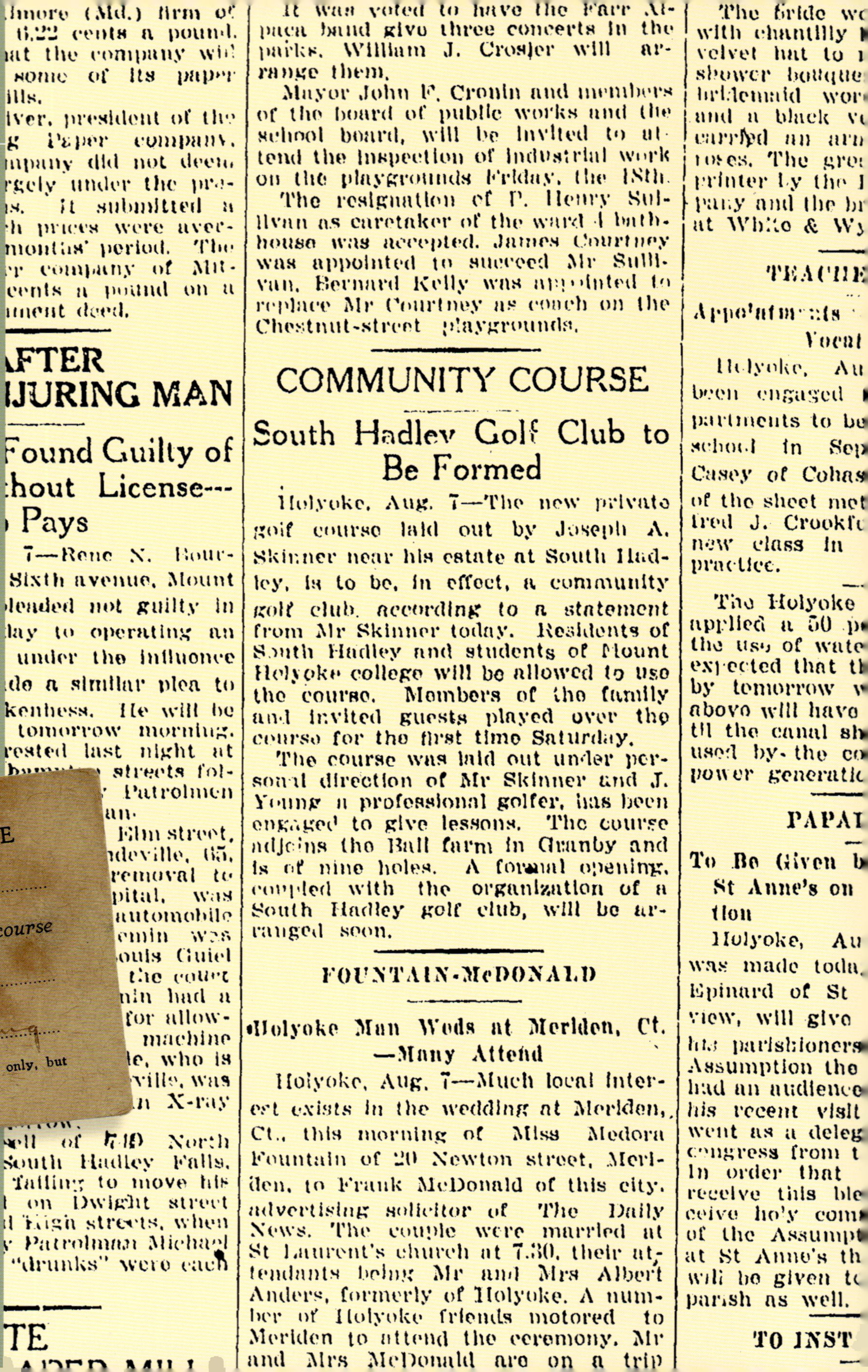

It was voted to have the Farr Alpaca band give three concerts in the parks. William J. Crosier will arrange them.

Mayor John F. Cronin and members of the board of public works and the school board, will be invited to attend the inspection of industrial work on the playgrounds Friday, the 18th.

The resignation of P. Henry Sullivan as caretaker of the ward 4 bathhouse was accepted. James Courtney was appointed to succeed Mr Sullivan. Bernard Kelly was appointed to replace Mr Courtney as coach on the Chestnut-street playgrounds.

COMMUNITY COURSE

South Hadley Golf Club to Be Formed

Holyoke, Aug. 7—The new private golf course laid out by Joseph A. Skinner near his estate at South Hadley, is to be, in effect, a community golf club, according to a statement from Mr Skinner today. Residents of South Hadley and students of Mount Holyoke college will be allowed to use the course. Members of the family and invited guests played over the course for the first time Saturday.

The course was laid out under personal direction of Mr Skinner and J. Young a professional golfer, has been engaged to give lessons. The course adjoins the Ball farm in Granby and is of nine holes. A formal opening, coupled with the organization of a South Hadley golf club, will be arranged soon.

FOUNTAIN-McDONALD

Holyoke Man Weds at Meriden, Ct. —Many Attend

Holyoke, Aug. 7—Much local interest exists in the wedding at Meriden, Ct., this morning of Miss Medora Fountain of 20 Newton street, Meriden, to Frank McDonald of this city, advertising solicitor of The Daily News. The couple were married at St Laurent's church at 7.30, their attendants being Mr and Mrs Albert Anders, formerly of Holyoke. A number of Holyoke friends motored to Meriden to attend the ceremony. Mr and Mrs McDonald are on a trip

...FTER ...JURING MAN

...Found Guilty of ...hout License--- ...Pays

TEACHE...

PAPAL...

TO INST...

Article from the *Springfield Republican,* noting that the first ball had been struck on Saturday, August 5, 1922, and a pass issued to play the course in 1927.
(Mount Holyoke College)

Elisabeth Skinner's scorecard from 1922

When the golf course opened, Joseph Skinner invited 40 of his friends to join. The price was $30 per year. The course was open to the public to play for a $1.00 daily fee. A Sunday school teacher, Joseph believed that everyone should be in church in the morning, so the course was not open for play until noon on Sundays. Twelve chimes from a nearby steeple signaled the start.

It's interesting to note Joseph's view of caddies. By not allowing them to work on Sundays, he was solicitous of them; however, players were not allowed to pay caddies more than the standard rate for their services, nor could they purchase golf balls from them. Was he protecting the players from being hustled by the little rapscallions?

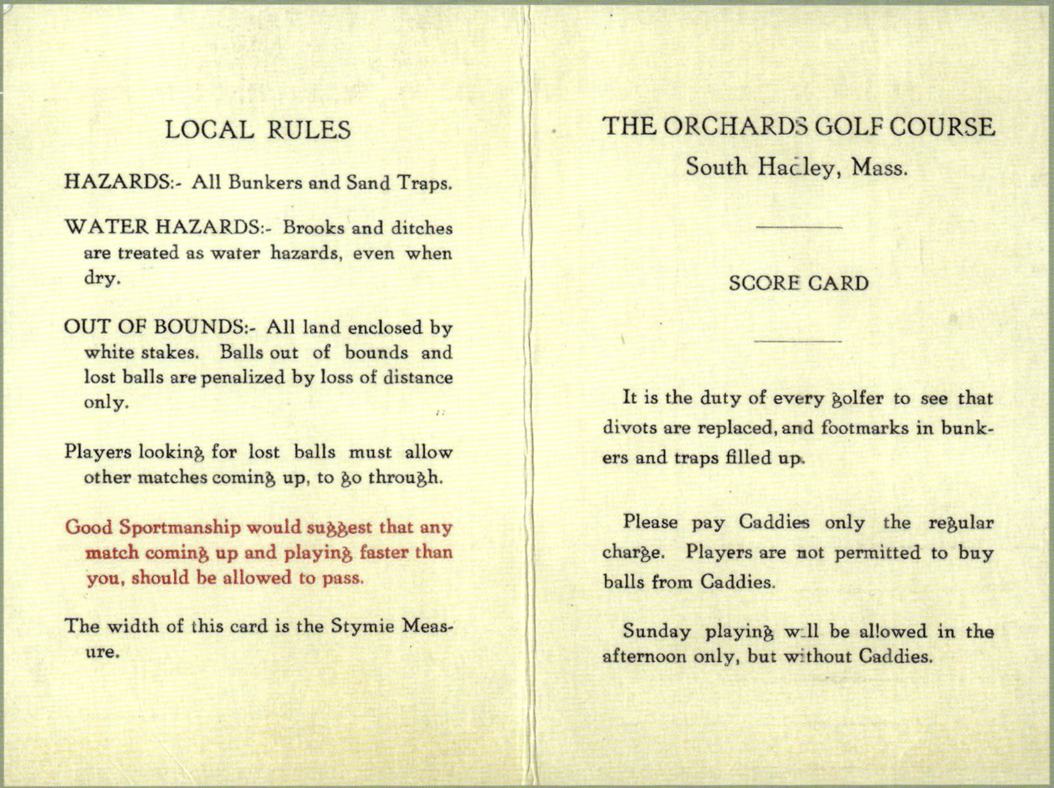

LOCAL RULES

HAZARDS:- All Bunkers and Sand Traps.

WATER HAZARDS:- Brooks and ditches are treated as water hazards, even when dry.

OUT OF BOUNDS:- All land enclosed by white stakes. Balls out of bounds and lost balls are penalized by loss of distance only.

Players looking for lost balls must allow other matches coming up, to go through.

Good Sportmanship would suggest that any match coming up and playing faster than you, should be allowed to pass.

The width of this card is the Stymie Measure.

THE ORCHARDS GOLF COURSE

South Hadley, Mass.

SCORE CARD

It is the duty of every golfer to see that divots are replaced, and footmarks in bunkers and traps filled up.

Please pay Caddies only the regular charge. Players are not permitted to buy balls from Caddies.

Sunday playing will be allowed in the afternoon only, but without Caddies.

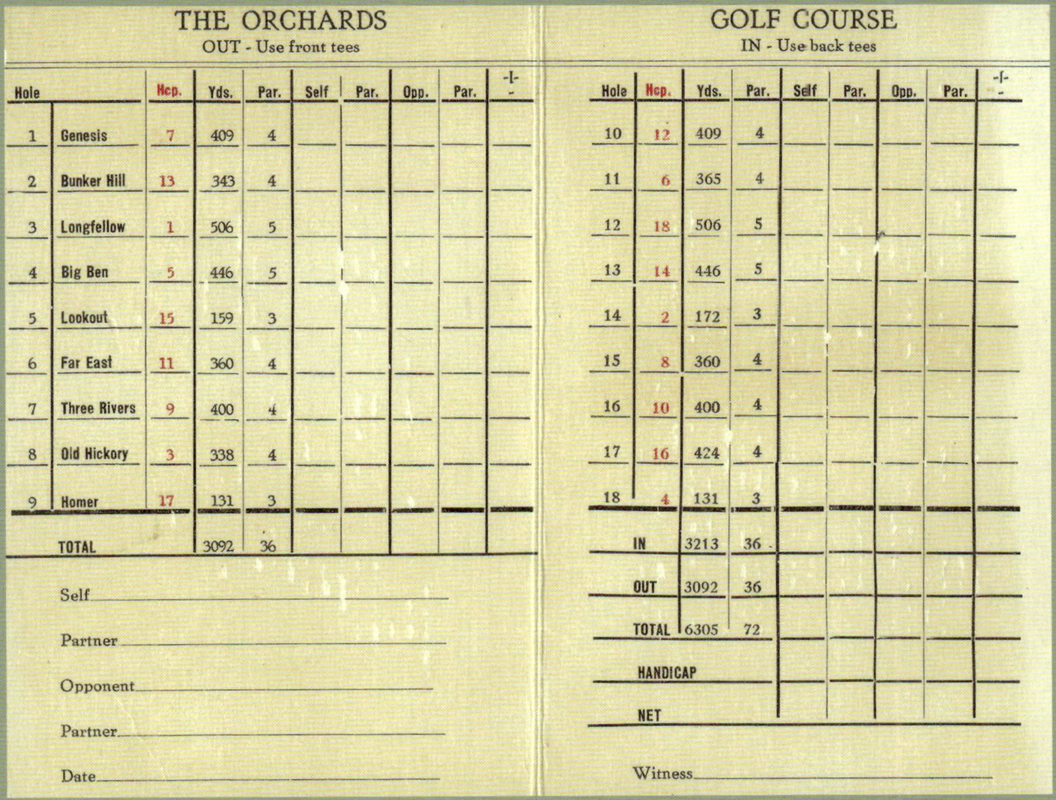

THE ORCHARDS GOLF COURSE

OUT - Use front tees

Hole		Hcp.	Yds.	Par.	Self	Par.	Opp.	Par.	-|-
1	Genesis	7	409	4					
2	Bunker Hill	13	343	4					
3	Longfellow	1	506	5					
4	Big Ben	5	446	5					
5	Lookout	15	159	3					
6	Far East	11	360	4					
7	Three Rivers	9	400	4					
8	Old Hickory	3	338	4					
9	Homer	17	131	3					
	TOTAL		3092	36					

Self

Partner

Opponent

Partner

Date

IN - Use back tees

Hole	Hcp.	Yds.	Par.	Self	Par.	Opp.	Par.	-|-
10	12	409	4					
11	6	365	4					
12	18	506	5					
13	14	446	5					
14	2	172	3					
15	8	360	4					
16	10	400	4					
17	16	424	4					
18	4	131	3					
IN		3213	36					
OUT		3092	36					
TOTAL		6305	72					
HANDICAP								
NET								

Witness

5
Building the Second Nine

"Great Caesar, there's no water!"

FIVE YEARS LATER, in 1927, Joseph decided he wanted to see another nine holes at The Orchards, so again he called Ross. As before, Walter Hatch brought a small crew of men and horses to the property, but unlike in 1921, he also brought a motorized tractor, which would shorten the construction time considerably. This time there's no doubt about Ross's presence at the course.

The property Joseph acquired for the second nine holes was better suited for a golf course than the first tract. It was hilly and mostly dry, attributes Ross favored. New holes were built, today's 4th, 5th, 6th, 7th, 8th, 12th, 13th, 14th, and 15th. In addition, two holes were reconfigured: the old 4th was modified to become the new 9th, and the old 7th became the 16th. A new par-3, the 17th hole, was constructed. Workers dug up a small pond and used the fill to build the green. The tee for the 18th was pushed down the hill, creating a long uphill finishing hole, ending near the clubhouse.

Hatch planted Kentucky bluegrass, which withstood cold weather better than other strains. Because its roots are shallow, it can't be cut shorter than one inch. This was intentional, since the fairways would be cut only once a week. They would be hard and fast in the summer; since there was no watering system, shots would travel forever. However, if a ball landed in the 6- to 12-inch rough, the penalty was dire. But at least the greens would be soft, since they'd be watered by hand. The new golf course was unquestionably finer than the original one. It was more interesting and challenging to play, its holes more diverse than those of the original nine.

Together Joseph and Ross walked the new property, looking for a place to relocate the clubhouse. A spot on the current 13th fairway, just short of the green, seemed ideal. It is the highest point on the property, with a spectacular view of the Holyoke mountain range. When Ross asked where he could tap into the water for the clubhouse, Joseph exclaimed, "Great Caesar, there's no water!" Because the town of South Hadley couldn't pump water to that elevation, the clubhouse would remain near Woodbridge Street.

Oh, but for a better pumping station, the clubhouse would have had the best view of any golf club in the Pioneer Valley. Instead, The Orchards would have to settle for being one of the best layouts in western Massachusetts.

A tractor similar to the one shown here in Pine Needles was used to construct the second nine holes. *(Tufts Archives)*

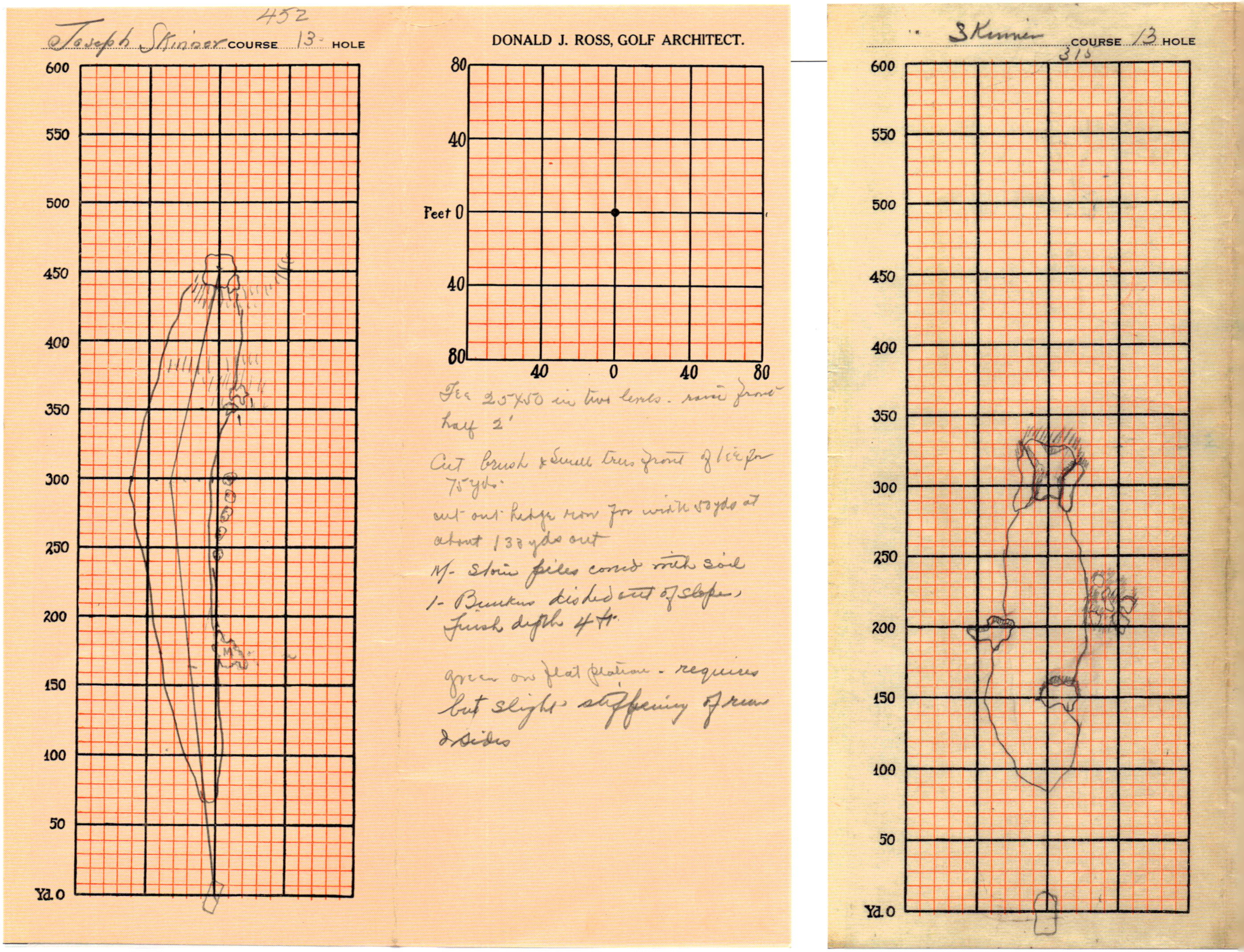

The 13th hole was envisioned to be a 315-yard uphill par-4 (right grid) with a new clubhouse located on the land beyond the green. It was to be the course's concluding hole; number 14 would likely have been the first. When Ross realized that water for the clubhouse couldn't be pumped to that location, he designed a 452-yard hole instead, which is how it plays today (left). *(Tufts Archives)*

DONALD J. ROSS, GOLF ARCHITECT.

SECTIONS

DONALD J. ROSS

GOLF COURSE ARCHITECTURE AND CONSTRUCTION

ASSOCIATES
WALTER B. HATCH
N. AMHERST, MASS.
J. B. McGOVERN
WYNNEWOOD, PA.

April 9, 1927.

Mr. Joseph A. Skinner,

Holyoke, Mass.

Dear Mr. Skinner;

I have gone over with Mr. Ross the matter of building the new nine holes for your golf course.

I enclose the details of a possible form of contract with the price therefor. We have figured as closely as is consistant with good work and feel sure we can give you an excellent addition to your present course. In the opinion of Mr. Ross and myself the new holes are of better golfing value than those which you now play.

On my return during the next week I shall be pleased to stop in and discuss the matter with you.

Very truly yours,

Walter B. Hatch

North Amherst, Mass.

Ross used a scorecard from 1922 to estimate the yardage of the expanded course; he ultimately changed five holes from this card (7, 8, 13, 17, 18).
(Tufts Archives)

with new 2nd nine added

THE ORCHARDS GOLF COURSE Skinners

OUT - Use front tees

Hole		Hcp.	Yds.	Par.	Self	Par.	Opp.	Par.	-I-
1	Genesis	7	409	4	409			172	
2	Bunker Hill	13	343	4	365			360	
3	Longfellow	1	506	5	506	new	hole	433	
4	Big Ben	5	new 446	hole 5	332	new	hole	315	
5	Lookout	15	new 159	hole 3	158	new	hole	407	
6	Far East	11	new 360	hole 4	363	new	hole	454	
7	Three Rivers	9	new 400	hole 4	424	Part	new	560	
8	Old Hickory	3	new 338	hole 4	225			424	
9	Homer	17	131	3	446			131	
TOTAL			3092	36	3228			3256	

3228
6,484

Self
Partner
Opponent
Partner
Date

IN - Use back tees

Hole	Hcp.	Yds.	Par.	Self.	Par.	Opp.	Par.	-I-
10	12	409	4					
11	6	365	4					
12	18	506	5					
13	14	446	5					
14	2	172	3					
15	8	360	4					
16	10	400	4					
17	16	424	4					
18	4	131	3					
IN		3213	36					
OUT		3092	36					
TOTAL		6305	72					
HANDICAP								
NET								

Witness

The course today.

Illustrations by Christopher Morris

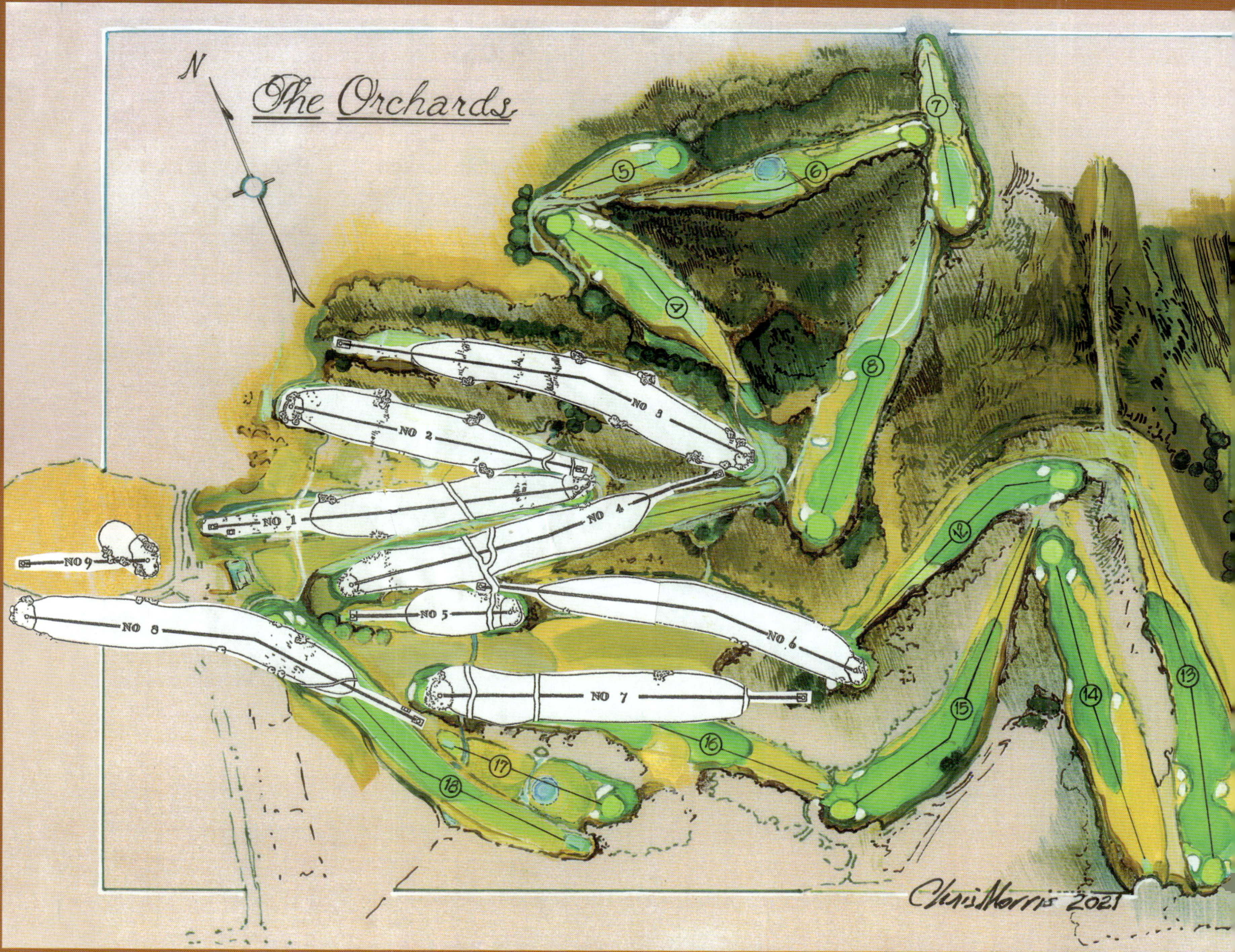

The white overlays show the original layout. Ten holes were added, three were modified, and one was eliminated in the final design.

Newly built Silverwood Terrace circa 1938.
(Mike Riley)

6
Elisabeth Skinner

"Father built the course because he wanted the townspeople to have a nice place to play."

ELISABETH SKINNER was born in Holyoke on December 17, 1891, the second of Joseph and Martha Skinner's four children. She was the most daring and athletic of her siblings. At age 14 she received one of the first driver's licenses issued to a woman by the State of Massachusetts. Normally sixteen was the minimum age, but because she spent her summers on a farm, she qualified.

Elisabeth was already playing golf at 13. She had a good swing, one that was honed at the Mt. Tom Golf Club in Holyoke, where her father was a charter member.

After high school she went to Vassar College, which her aunts had attended. She excelled outside the classroom, but it wasn't at golf. Vassar wouldn't have its own course until 1930. Instead, she was first violin in the college orchestra and she ran track. There's little doubt that Joseph encouraged his daughter to set her own path in life.

After graduation, Elisabeth returned to South Hadley to live with her family. Her two sisters and brother would eventually marry and move out of the house, but Elisabeth remained at home. When not playing golf, she helped care for her mother, whose painful rheumatoid arthritis was slowly turning her into an invalid. There were no steroid shots or antirheumatic drugs at the time, only experimental treatments that did little to help. Eventually Martha became wheelchair-bound and rarely left her home.

One has to wonder how Elisabeth reacted when she learned of her father's plans to build a golf course across the street. He loved South Hadley, so it was probably another of his investments in the community, a park everyone might enjoy. However, she knew her father would do anything to help her pursue her ambitions, so maybe it was meant for her. Whatever the reason, there's little doubt that proximity to the course helped her become a champion.

***Lady Astor Playing Golf at North Berwick, Scotland*, by Sir John Lavery.** *(Bridgeman Art)*

Elisabeth became an attentive student of Jimmy Young, The Orchards' first golf professional, who was an excellent player and a patient teacher. They would often play with Ray Roberts, who said of Elisabeth, "She was a very long hitter for a woman." She must have been, because she could drive the brook on the first hole from the tee beside the pro shop. Once, she participated in a long-drive contest, and her 222-yard smash won the event. It was an impressive shot, given the equipment of the day. One-time caddy Howard Warner said of her swing, "She would waggle an ever-lengthening back swing until she could see the club head out of the corner of her left eye." Many players with hickory shafts had a similar swing. It generated a lot of whip for power, but at the expense of accuracy. Elisabeth's drives, however, usually found the fairway. She once played a round with Jock Hutchison, a professional player, who said she had "extraordinary control."

Elisabeth wanted to play against accomplished competitors, so she frequently invited men from outside the Club to join her. Always eager to improve her game, she wasn't afraid to ask them for advice. She built a putting green and a couple of holes behind the family estate on which to practice. These holes were long enough to accommodate her mashie, a seven iron in modern parlance. She made history in 1930 when she played with Jimmy Young in a pro-am tournament, the first time a woman had competed against men in western Massachusetts.

Before long, she was winning local and regional tournaments, bringing home trophies from Mt. Tom, Longmeadow Country Club, and many more. Her most prestigious prize was the Endicott Cup, an annual competition for champion golfers from Massachusetts, Connecticut, and Rhode Island. To win it once would have been a great achievement, but she did it twice, in 1930 and 1931.

Elisabeth and Joseph in 1945. *(Bill Armistead)*

From left: William Skinner II, Joe Kirkwood, Joseph Skinner, and Alex McKinzie in 1932. *(Bill Armistead)*

Elisabeth's fondest memory of The Orchards, she said, was in 1932, when she played with Joe Kirkwood, a professional golfer and trick-shot artist from Australia. No doubt inspired by his presence, she shot a 74 that day, her lowest score at The Orchards. It set a course record for a woman that wouldn't be surpassed for 41 years.

After many years of suffering, Martha Skinner passed away in 1934. As much as they loved her, Joseph and Elisabeth must have felt some relief when the burden of caring for her was lifted. They traveled extensively, to Scotland, to Egypt, to South Africa. They found the time they spent abroad immensely enjoyable.

It was around 1939 that Elisabeth fell while skating on the Mount Holyoke College pond, fracturing her wrist. The pain remained when she ventured onto the course the following season. Her first shot didn't make it past the stand of pine trees on the left side of the opening hole, a distance of

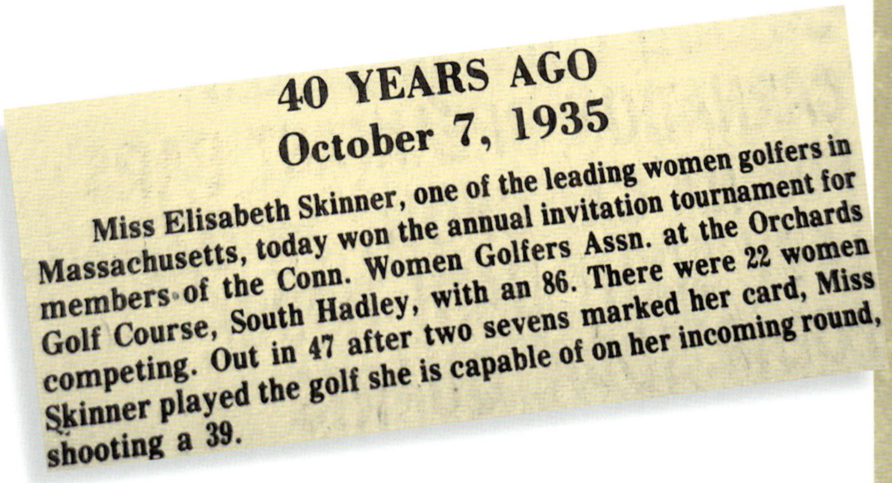

40 YEARS AGO
October 7, 1935

Miss Elisabeth Skinner, one of the leading women golfers in Massachusetts, today won the annual invitation tournament for members of the Conn. Women Golfers Assn. at the Orchards Golf Course, South Hadley, with an 86. There were 22 women competing. Out in 47 after two sevens marked her card, Miss Skinner played the golf she is capable of on her incoming round, shooting a 39.

Elisabeth had a long backswing, like that of Englishman Harry Vardon. *(Bridgeman Art)*

LOW GROSS
WON BY
ELISABETH SKINNER
1930

about 150 yards which she had easily reached before. She walked to the ball, put it in her pocket, and left the course. Elisabeth's interest in the game began to wane when the pain failed to go away. It never would. She stopped playing competitively, and the number of trips she made across the street declined. Whenever she did play, she would often limit herself to nine holes.

It was at this time that Joseph decided to part with the course. He asked Jimmy Young if he would be interested in buying it, but Jimmy couldn't arrange the financing. Joseph was prepared to donate The Orchards to Mount Holyoke College when a friend, Judge Russell Davenport, thought it better if he sold the course. In 1941 he offered it to the College for $25,000.

Opposite, clockwise from the left: Elisabeth's golf clubs *(Michael Carroll)*; a woman in attire that was common at the turn of the century *(Bridgeman Art)*; the Endicott Cup *(WGBY)*; and a trophy from Mt. Tom. *(WGBY)* Right: Elisabeth at 13 years of age. *(Wistariahurst Museum)*

MOUNT HOLYOKE
OUTING CLUB

7
Mount Holyoke College

"Go where no one else will go, do what no one else will do."
—Mary Lyon

THE IDEA OF HIGHER education for young women in 1837 wasn't merely progressive, it was almost revolutionary. Victorian thinking about women's roles in society prevailed: women didn't need a college degree, since their path in life would be as homemakers or domestic workers. Educator Mary Lyon challenged that notion when she opened Mount Holyoke Female Seminary that year. She envisioned larger roles for women, and they had to be educated if they were to participate in the changing society. Academics were stressed at the new school, with math and the sciences at the forefront. No domestic training classes were taught. Theology was an important part of the curriculum, its teachers emphasizing Christian values of humility, charity, and virtue. The school also preached the benefits of physical exercise.

Lyon wanted to enroll young women from families of all economic backgrounds, not just the upper class, so tuition was kept at an affordable level. Although the seminary had a small endowment when it opened its doors thanks to Lyon's endless letter-writing for support, to make ends meet, students were required to clean and cook. Emily Dickinson, who grew up in nearby Amherst, was a member of the class of 1849.

South Hadley at this time was a small manufacturing community producing buttons, leather, and some textile goods. Its prosperity relied on the boat traffic that navigated the South Hadley canal, which had been built at the end of the century to bypass the falls on the Connecticut River. When railroads became the dominant means of transportation, traffic along the canal diminished, and by the time the canal closed, in

Members of the Outing Club, circa 1958. *(Mount Holyoke College)*; **Above: College president Mary Woolley.** *(Mount Holyoke College)*

Mount Holyoke College. *(Mount Holyoke College)*

Roswell Ham, who succeeded Woolley in 1937. *(Mount Holyoke College)*

1863, so had many of South Hadley's businesses.

In 1893 the seminary softened its emphasis on religion and was renamed Mount Holyoke College. Then, in 1900, it took a transformative step when it hired 38-year-old Mary Woolley as president. Young as she was, the board likely hired her because of the changes she had made to the curriculum at Wellesley College. Woolley believed the goal of any women's college was to provide the best education possible; everything else was secondary. An educated woman could pursue anything in life and be successful, while an uneducated woman could not. The College needed to raise its standards of admission and improve the caliber of its faculty to fulfill her lofty mission. Thus Woolley brought in scholars from top-flight universities, enticing them with high salaries and fellowships. She emphasized fundraising, meeting with leaders from Wellesley, Smith, and Vassar to develop money-raising strategies. In her long tenure as president, she would grow

the College's endowment tenfold and add more than a dozen buildings to the campus.

After Woolley stepped down, in 1936, the board voted to replace her with a man, a move that was totally unexpected. Women had led the College since its founding and many alumnae were outraged at the announcement of Woolley's successor. Their resentment had nothing to do with the candidate himself; it was just that he was a male. By taking this step, they believed the board was tacitly admitting that women were inferior to men. It was, they said, a blow to women's advancement, especially because it was occurring at Mount Holyoke, the institution that had done so much for the feminist movement. They hoped the new appointee would decline the position in order to avoid the disruption that would surely follow.

Eventually the furor over the announcement died down, and in 1937, Roswell Ham became the College's twelfth

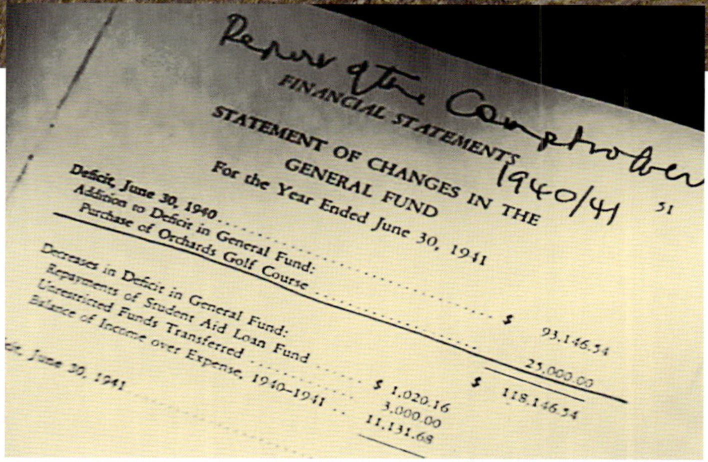

Report of the Comptroller 1940/41

FINANCIAL STATEMENTS

STATEMENT OF CHANGES IN THE GENERAL FUND

For the Year Ended June 30, 1941

51

Deficit, June 30, 1940 .... $ 93,146.54

Addition to Deficit in General Fund:

Purchase of Orchards Golf Course 25,000.00

$ 118,146.54

Decreases in Deficit in General Fund:

Repayments of Student Aid Loan Fund .... $ 1,020.16

Unrestricted Funds Transferred 3,000.00

Balance of Income over Expense, 1940–1941 .. 11,131.68

...cit, June 30, 1941

A record of the purchase of the course in 1941. ***(WBGY)***

president. He continued Woolley's focus on fundraising, doubling the endowment by the time he retired in 1957, and he grew the physical plant. The remodeling of the 1893 church was the first of many such improvements.

As the 1940s began, there would be another expansion of the College's physical assets, this one of a different order. When Joseph Skinner offered to sell his golf course to Mount Holyoke, it was an offer Ham couldn't refuse.

With the Pro on the 18th green

8

Jimmy and Minnie Young

Lives Lived at The Orchards, *By Mary Chaffee*

JAMES DUFF (JIMMY) YOUNG was born in 1889 in Strathkinness, a village on the western edge of St. Andrews, golf's birthplace. Golf had been played at St. Andrews since the 1400s, and it grew to be the dominant club in British golf and the standard for courses worldwide. Jimmy's religious parents discouraged his interest in golf, but his athleticism, and the proximity of the St. Andrews links, prevailed. He was caddying and playing golf by age 12, as well as participating in soccer, curling, and distance running. When his workday as a clerk ended, he headed to St. Andrews. "I used to race from my job to the course at five and then play golf until we had to follow the ball with our ears. Sometimes it would be eleven o'clock before we called it quits," Young said.

In 1910, at age 20, Jimmy Young sailed from Scotland to the United States. In short order he obtained American citizenship, served as a U.S. Army sergeant in World War I, and found clerical work in Holyoke. Jimmy's employers described him as "able, industrious and efficient" and a "first class office man."

Not long before his 30th birthday, Jimmy and some Scottish friends attended a dance at Holyoke's Caledonian Club, the city's center of social activity for Scottish immigrants. A 20-year-old lass from Glasgow named Mary Roy Fox, known as Minnie, caught his interest. Armed with the equivalent of an eighth-grade education, teenaged Minnie had found work at a milliner's and at Joseph Skinner's silk mills before she met Jimmy. Jimmy walked Minnie home that night and they married a year later, in 1920.

The newlywed Youngs heard of economic opportunity in Michigan's new automobile industry and left Holyoke for Detroit. Jimmy found work there, but it was not long before an economic downturn ended his job after only eight months. Encounters with two fellow Scots would soon propel Jimmy Young into a nearly 40-year-long golf career. In Detroit Jimmy had met golf star Jock

Jimmy Young was one of the first PGA professionals to teach golf to women. ***(Mount Holyoke College)***

Top: Jock Hutchison, Jimmy Young, and Johnny Banks *(Bill Young)*; **Above: Jimmy with his three children, Margie, Jimmy Jr., in uniform, and Billy.** *(Bill Young)*

Hutchison from St. Andrews. He'd won the 1920 PGA Championship and would win the British Open the following year, and he urged Jimmy to turn pro as soon as possible.

Jimmy and Minnie returned to Holyoke, where another Scot opened a door for Jimmy. Johnny Banks, a boyhood friend of Jimmy's from St. Andrews, was a club professional. In 1921 he told Jimmy that Joseph Skinner planned to build a golf course near his South Hadley home and advised Jimmy to apply for the new course's club pro position. Joseph Skinner hired Jimmy. His first duties were to help Donald Ross's team lay out the new course. The Orchards' first nine holes were ready for play in 1922, and Jimmy began his duties as club professional, instructor, bookkeeper, greenskeeper, and pro shop manager. In the winter he worked as an accountant in Skinner's silk mills. During the playing season, Young was required to play golf with Skinner family members. Most rounds were with Elisabeth Skinner, who was becoming one of New England's top women amateur golfers.

Just beyond The Orchards' 1st tee stood a wooden dwelling that Jimmy and Minnie moved into in 1924, as Minnie was about to deliver Jimmy Young, Jr., the couple's first child. Minnie had known only city life and had felt isolated in South Hadley, but her life at The Orchards became busy as her family grew and she joined Jimmy working at the course. Minnie gave birth to the Youngs' second child, Marjorie (Margie), in 1927 and their third child, William (Billy), in 1937. The children grew up on the course, helping in the pro shop and with course maintenance. The boys also caddied under their father's careful supervision.

Joseph Skinner invited Donald Ross back to The Orchards in 1927 to extend the course to 18 holes. Jimmy considered the course the best in the area. The Orchards provided an environment where both he and Elisabeth Skinner excelled. Jimmy dominated western Massachusetts golf by the mid-1930s. Sports columnist Gerry Finn wrote, "In his prime Jimmy won virtually everything in sight." In 1924 Jimmy played in the USGA's National Open Golf Championship eastern sectional. Other players teeing off there included Walter Hagen and Gene Sarazen, two of golf's stars in the roaring twenties. Young was elected to the Professional Golfers' Association of America (PGA) in 1927. He won the Western Massachusetts Open in 1929 and in 1936 when it was held at The Orchards.

In 1935 Jimmy shot a 66 at The Orchards, tying the course record set by Australian star Joe Kirkwood. "I expected to win, and I wasn't satisfied with anything else," Young said. Reporter Victor Wall wrote in 1949 that Jimmy had qualified for the national PGA tournament seven times, set a course record 67 in a national tour event at Metacomet Golf Club in Providence, Rhode Island, and won tournaments across New England. When asked why he hadn't joined the PGA tour, Jimmy said that he had a job during the Great Depression, and a wife and children to support.

For a period, Jimmy lost his competitive drive. Jimmy Jr. was an Army Air Corps B-24 Liberator pilot in World War II and was shot down by the Nazis during a raid on Ploesti, Romania, in 1943. His father did not play competitive golf during the two-year period Jimmy Jr. was reported missing.

Top: The clubhouse, date unknown. *(Mount Holyoke College)*
Above: Jimmy on the first tee; the Youngs' house is in the distance. *(Bill Young)*

Jimmy Jr., Tom Tait, Ray Roberts, Jimmy Young, Howard Warner, and Tom Chaffee. *(Bill Young)*

World War II Army service, Tom came home and married the Youngs' daughter, Margie.

In 1957 his son Bill won the New England College Golf Championship as a sophomore at the University of Massachusetts at Amherst and the NCAA Long Drive Championship the same year. He had started playing golf just five years earlier, but when he began he'd turned to his father for instruction.

Jimmy was honored at the 1958 Western Massachusetts Tee Party, an annual celebration of regional golf talent. His former pupil Elisabeth Skinner, who generally avoided large events, joined the 150 well-wishers honoring Young's 36 years of leadership at The Orchards.

Army officials knocked on the Youngs' door in 1945, and Bill Young, then 10, could see his mother's fear. But the news was good: Jimmy Jr. had been liberated from a Nazi prison camp. Bill ran up to the clubhouse to find his dad, yelling "Jimmy's alive!" Thereafter Jimmy Sr.'s competitive spirit returned to stay. In 1956 at age 66, he teamed with Ray Roberts to win the Western Massachusetts Pro-Club Champion tournament. His son Bill caddied for him one day at The Orchards when Jimmy was in his mid-sixties and the weather was "a monsoon." Playing with local pros, Jimmy told his son, "They will never catch me," and he was right.

When Mount Holyoke College began offering golf instruction in the 1930s, Jimmy taught several classes a day, becoming one of the first PGA professionals to teach women golfers.

Jimmy was the first western Massachusetts pro to use steel-shafted clubs, in 1926. The transition from wood to steel meant that clubs were heavier and golfers needed more of them, which ensured that caddies became a vital part of life at golf clubs. Tom and Bill Chaffee, brothers who lived near the course, were caddies there in the 1930s and 1940s. After

While Jimmy's career thrived, Minnie combined her roles as housewife and mother with work at The Orchards. When Jimmy played or taught, Minnie managed the pro shop. When a member planned a banquet at the Orchards but forgot to hire food servers, Minnie raced over to pitch in as a waitress. During World War II, the club's laundry service stopped deliveries due to gas rationing. Minnie washed all the club towels by hand. A few stories offer glimpses into the Youngs' marriage and their wit. When Minnie served a dinner Jimmy didn't care for and he expressed his displeasure, Minnie replied, "Do you always shoot par?" And one day while practicing her golf swing near their home, Minnie hit a ball that hit the Youngs' cat. Alarmed, she ran to the pro shop to tell her husband. Said Jimmy, "Don't worry, Minnie. The way you swing, you couldn't hurt him."

When Jimmy approached age 70 in 1960, he retired after 38 years as The Orchards' first club professional. In retirement, the Youngs traveled twice to Scotland so Jimmy could watch the Open. Mount Holyoke College gave the couple golf privileges for life at The Orchards, and they enjoyed many rounds.

Jimmy died in 1967. The day of his funeral, David Adams, a former *Holyoke Transcript-Telegram* reporter, was stopped by a lengthy funeral procession in South Hadley. When he learned that it was Jimmy Young's funeral, for whom he had caddied years earlier, Adams wrote to his mother, "I am sorry to hear of the death of Jim Young, Sr. I hope you will tell Mrs. Young that there are hundreds of boys and men who will remember him as kind but firm, a man among men, who set a good example for many. It was a coveted thing to caddy for Jim, and I am sure that most of us recall him as a man who knew how to behave like a champion." The Orchards honors Jimmy annually with the annual James D. Young Member-Guest Tournament.

Minnie lived on 30 years after Jimmy's death, cooking Scottish meat pies and playing golf until she was 85. The Orchards honored her with an annual tournament in her name. She died at 97 in 1997 and "The Bonnie Banks o' Loch Lomond," a Scottish folk song, was played at her funeral. Jimmy and Minnie are buried together, less than a mile from The Orchards, at South Hadley's Evergreen Cemetery with their daughter Margie. It's a peaceful, wooded spot in the college town that became their adopted home thanks to an opportunity provided by Joseph Skinner.

Mary Chaffee is the daughter of Marjorie Young Chaffee and Tom Chaffee, and is the granddaughter of Jimmy and Minnie Young. Raised near The Orchards, she is a retired Navy captain now living on Cape Cod and working as a public official.

Minnie Young with friends in the mid-1990s. *(Margie Riley)*
Below, Minnie on the first tee. *(Bill Young)*

The Old Course in 1901, **by William Frazer.**
(Bridgeman Art)

9

Spalding

"Spalding first made Calamity Janes for the market in 1931." —*Bobby Jones*

TODAY THE SPALDING NAME is best known for its basketballs. However, going back to its 1876 founding in Chicago, A. G. Spalding & Brothers made every kind of sports equipment imaginable, including baseballs, tennis balls, bowling balls, hockey pucks, punching bags, fencing blades, and many other items.

In 1891 James Naismith was teaching physical education at the YMCA training school in Springfield, Massachusetts, when he created a new game. Shortly after Spalding purchased a plant in nearby Chicopee Falls in 1893, he approached the company to improve the ball he had been using. It wasn't long before Spalding made the first basketball. Two years later, William Morgan, a former student of Naismith, also developed a new sport, this one in a YMCA gym in Holyoke. He tried using a basketball for this game but found it too heavy, so he approached Spalding to make a lighter version. Thus in 1895, Spalding made the first volleyball.

Spalding began manufacturing golf clubs in its Chicopee Falls plant in 1905, to complement its golf ball production. The shafts were made of hickory, the standard material at that time, and the legendary Bobby Jones was the company's spokesman. Sixteen years later the Bristol Steel Company in Connecticut brought the golf club into the modern era when it developed a seamless tubular shaft made of steel.

Spalding came out with its version of the metal shaft in 1926, and Jimmy Young was one of its first customers. Whenever a member at The Orchards needed new clubs, Jimmy would drive him to Chicopee to select the ones he wanted. Elisabeth Skinner, however, saw no need to abandon her hickory clubs, which she had come to master.

There's a curious story about the golf ball Elisabeth used on October 21, 1929, the day she had a hole-in-one on the 17th. Howard Warner, her caddy that day, confirmed that she had an ace, but the ball sitting on the brass

Manufacturing golf clubs at the Chicopee Falls plant in the 1930s. ***(Callaway Golf)***

stand, known as the "double dot" Top Flite, wasn't sold to the public until 1931. How could that be? Well, Spalding began promoting its new double dot line in 1929, handing out samples to golf professionals, hoping they would buy them when they were released for sale. Jimmy Young was probably given a couple dozen balls, and he gave one to Elisabeth to try. There's no doubt she loved the new version.

Clockwise from below: Elisabeth's hole-in-one ball. *(Bill Armistead)*; **the Chicopee Falls plant.** *(Callaway Golf)*; **an iron owned by Jimmy.** *(Michael Carroll)*

Inspecting and finishing golf balls.
(Callaway Golf)

6

10
Caddies

"You did so well with that club, use it again."

SINCE THE EARLY DAYS of golf, caddies have been an integral part of the game. In 18th-century Scotland, porters—or caddies as they were known—carried water to homes in the villages. It wasn't long before their services were extended to the links. Most caddies were boys hauling unbundled clubs for noblemen and -women. As the game moved to America, caddies worked for those of less noble means as well.

In the 1920s, the rate for a caddy at The Orchards was only 50 cents per round, plus a 25- to 50-cent tip. There were about 10 boys caddying for the 40 members in 1922. As the membership grew, so did the number of boys looking for work. At its peak, about 50 boys could be called upon to carry members' bags. New caddies were called chippees. It took a year or so to become a full caddy, a rank that was significant because the better tippers were assigned to them.

Under Jimmy Young's management, caddies did far more than tote clubs. He taught them to go into water hazards to find balls, not simply poke around the edges. He had them strap small boards with nails protruding from the bottom onto their shoes to aerate the greens twice a year. Caddies tended to the greens and bunkers as well. Before there were herbicides, greens had to be manicured by hand to remove weeds. The boys were rewarded for their pruning with the privilege to play nine holes for each green they treated. Jimmy made sure they had done their job well before granting those passes.

During the Depression the money a caddy earned was not insignificant. One-time caddy and future member Herb Crossland recalled that if he missed a caddy assignment his family would be upset: "We were pretty poor, and my caddy pay went into the house money."

When pull carts arrived in the mid-1940s, the burden of carrying one's bag was lifted and calls for caddies started to decline. Although members had to read the greens and fish their own errant shots from the water, it was a way to save money.

As the date for the 1948 Eastern Air Force Tournament at The Orchards approached, organizers placed ads in local newspapers to find boys to help. Some who showed up knew nothing about the game. After hitting a long drive onto the fairway of the par-4 8th hole, one player asked his caddy

***Putting on the Sixth Green*, by William Edwin.** *(Bridgeman Art)*

what club he should use next. The boy replied, "You did so well with that club, use it again."

When motorized carts arrived at the Club in 1960, the number of caddies dwindled further. Some members decided they would rather ride than make the hilly trek. By 1990, caddies only showed up by appointment.

Today, many golf courses require players to rent carts. This brings in revenue and, because of the increased distances between greens and tees, improves the pace of play. At The Orchards, only 32 percent of those who played in 2020 used a motorized cart, which is low for the region. The Club's membership consists largely of traditional golfers,

The scorecard on the lower right was witnessed by Roswell Ham, president of MHC. ***(Mount Holyoke College)***

Front row from left to right: Bill Young, Max the dog, Jimmy Young; Middle row: Jack Crooke, an unknown O'Connor, Bill Roberts,

who recognize the benefits of walking. But there are no caddies. Members either carry their own bags or use push carts when they aren't riding. Only the wealthy and historic clubs have retained their caddy programs.

Sadly, something that was once so fundamental to the game is slowly disappearing.

Bill Chaffee, Henry Stahlman, Steve Bys, unknown; Third row: Peter Thomson, Bill Whelan, Tom Chaffee, Jim Young Jr., rest of row unknown. *(Bill Young)*

Mary Queen of Scots

Mary Queen of Scots is thought to have coined the word "caddy." The story is probably apocryphal, but because she was a queen who enjoyed the game, it became part of golfing lore.

Mary Stuart was an infant when she acceded to the Scottish throne in 1542, so she spent her childhood in France. Given her noble rank, she was entitled to have military aides, or cadets, carry whatever she wanted transported. When she learned to play pall-mall, an early version of croquet, a cadet carried her mallets around the court. The French pronunciation for cadet is ca-*day*, but Mary called him caddy, which stuck when she returned to her home near St. Andrews.

Her love of golf eventually damaged her reputation. Instead of mourning the death of her husband, Lord Darnley, she was seen golfing a few days after his demise. Suspicions only grew when, one month later, she married the alleged murderer.

(Michael Carroll)

Part Two

Pros, Cons, and Lyons

The Weather
CLOUDY, COOL TONIGHT; MILDER TOMORROW

Springfield Daily News

5 O'CLOCK LATE NEWS

75th Year, No. 210 — ESTABLISHED IN 1880 BY CHARLES J. BELLAMY — SPRINGFIELD, MASS., TUESDAY EVENING, NOVEMBER 1, 1955 — FIVE CENTS — FORTY PAGES

L. I. GOLF 'HOAX' REVEALED

With the confession by one of the winning pair in a September golf tournament on Long Island that both his identity and credentials were falsified, a scandal that took six weeks of investigation to uncover was today revealed to involve Western Massachusetts golfers.

The probe was carried out by the Deepdale Country Club of Long Island, acting with the New York World-Telegram and Sun, following an invitation tournament held on the week end of Sept. 18-19.

Winning the event were two golfers named on the entry list as Billy Roberts of Amherst and Richard Vitali of The Orchards at South Hadley. Investigation by the club and newspaper proved that Charles

11

Deepdale

"I did wrong, morally and golf-wise." —*Bill Roberts*

THE NAME ALONE connotes scandal. Over the years, some golf clubs held calcuttas, a form of gambling, in which members placed bets on amateur golfers who competed in tournaments they sponsored. The betting was meant to provide extra excitement; those who picked the winning team split the pot with the players. But when the pots became substantial, as they occasionally did at wealthy clubs, these events weren't simply fun competitions, they were dead serious.

No one knows for sure how it happened that Bill Roberts, a member of The Orchards and son of Ray Roberts, its longest-standing member, received an invitation to compete in a calcutta tournament at Deepdale Golf Club in Manhasset, New York, in 1955. When he filled out his application, Roberts listed fellow Club member Dick Vitali as his partner. When Vitali told Roberts he didn't want to go, Roberts persuaded Bud Helmar, an excellent player from Springfield, to take his place.

Computers were not around at the time to check players' handicaps, so what you reported to the official scorer mattered. Roberts was a three handicap, as was Helmar, but Roberts gave himself a 17 and Helmar an 18. Since Vitali's name was still on the official scoresheet, Helmar played under that name. It was no surprise that they won the two-day event by five strokes. It would have been a greater margin had they not played like a couple of hackers on the 36th hole in a last-minute attempt not to arouse suspicion. Their gambit worked, and they walked away with almost $4,000. Not long afterward, Helmar wrote a "conscience-stricken" letter to the president of Deepdale, explaining what had happened and expressing his apologies. Six weeks later, the story made the national news.

As a result, the USGA revoked the amateur status of both Roberts and Helmar, and no USGA-recognized golf club would allow them to play. A few years later Helmar regained his playing privileges, but Roberts never did. Because Roberts and Vitali were members of The Orchards, the Club's name was bandied about in the national news for a couple of months, the kind of publicity it wished it had never endured.

Oh, Calcutta!

Entrance to Deepdale Golf Club, where Dwight Eisenhower often played. *(John Sabino)*

12

The 1960s

"Dan Webster made some good changes." —*Frank Guzek*

After Jimmy Young's retirement, Dan Webster became head golf professional. Young had been at the Club for 38 years, which is a long time for anyone to serve in this capacity, so it must have been quite an adjustment for the membership when Webster walked through the clubhouse door. If numbers tell the story, though, they quickly embraced its new pro. There were 200 members at The Orchards in the early 1960s, a record. Annual dues were $100, which was still very affordable, the pro shop tripled in size, and the storage room was revamped. Webster brought golf carts to the course for the first time and built bridges over the brooks to accommodate them, and the food shack made its debut on the 10th tee, so players wouldn't have to walk up the steep hill for a sandwich at the turn.

Don Young was the course superintendent, which relieved Webster of a chore that had been one of Jimmy Young's responsibilities. Working with Webster, he drew up a five-year plan to restore the ponds on the 6th and 17th holes and renovate four tees. An underground irrigation system would be built, reaching all the greens and teeing areas.

Like his predecessor, Webster gave golf lessons to Mount Holyoke College students. He also encouraged the female members of the Club to form a group, and their numbers increased over the decade. This was a major step for The Orchards, since women hadn't received much attention in the past. Ada Lawler would be the Club's inaugural Women's Champion in 1963.

More tournaments were held than in the decade before, both within the Club and beyond it. In 1961 Webster established an annual 10-man tournament with UMass and Amherst. The Orchards won the first meeting, led by its captain, Mitzie Twardzik. In 1962, Joe Price won the Tait Memorial, and Les Kahan took home the Mt. Holyoke Trophy.

And there were prodigies. In 1962, 15-year-old Club member Mitch Alexander was the youngest person to win the Western Massachusetts schoolboy championship. He would return to glory seven years later when, at age 22, he won the Jimmy Young Member-Guest Tournament. The Jimmy Young Tournament quickly became a premiere event in the Pioneer Valley. The decade also witnessed the end of an era when Ray Roberts won the last of his eight Club Championships, in 1969.

Dan Webster on the left with Jimmy Young and Doug Sanders circa 1963. ***(Bill Young)***

Club member Frank Guzek spoke favorably of Webster although another member recalls that he almost left The Orchards after one year because he didn't feel welcomed by its pro. That would change as the decade came to a close and a new golf professional took Webster's place.

Below, the snack shack and an early golf cart. *(Margie Riley)* **Bottom: Dan Webster watching Martha Kraus, Class of 1963.** *(Mount Holyoke College)*

(Michael Carroll)

Ray Roberts

No person had a longer association with The Orchards than Ray Roberts. He was raised in a house next to the 2nd green, and he knew the property before it was a golf course. He watched Walter Hatch's crew build the first nine holes in 1922 and the second nine five years later, and he helped plant the pine trees along the fairways.

Ray was a baseball player and didn't pick up a golf club until he was 25. Because he worked at night, he could play during the day, which he did most days of the week. Within just a few years he became a superb golfer, so good in fact that Jimmy Young and Elisabeth Skinner often invited him to join their daily game. Ray won the Club Championship eight times, and he was still shooting his age or better when he was in his eighties.

Ray was known to push the rules—he often carried a foot wedge in his bag—and he was notoriously cheap. For all the years Bob Bontempo knew Ray, he cannot recall him spending a dime at the pro shop. Instead, Ray would play with used balls and broken tees he found on the course.

When he finally stopped playing, Ray would hang out at the Club and chat with friends. As was the case with many long-time members, The Orchards was his second home.

13

Bob Bontempo

"He was like family to me."

THE SON OF A LEADING GOLF PRO in western Massachusetts, Bob Bontempo seemed destined to go into the family business. His father, Henry, was the head professional at Franconia Golf Course in Springfield for 40 years and was one of the best players in the region. Bob had a successful career of his own. He was a standout junior player, winning a citywide tournament in Springfield and two Massachusetts championships. He played for the University of North Carolina golf team, was the pro at Twin Hills Country Club in Longmeadow, and at age 30 became head professional at The Orchards.

Bob with trophy from 1988. *(MassLive)*

Bob started at the Club in 1970 and stayed for 25 years. The Orchards experienced some difficult times during his tenure, although none were of his making. The gradual deterioration of the course was most notable. But there were happy times as well, including the collegiate tournaments in 1973, 1979, and 1980, the 1987 Girls' Junior Championship, the many MGA events, the annual Jimmy Young Four Ball, and 20 pro-am tournaments.

Bob single-handedly changed the spirit of the Club, which he called Orchards National. "We have pride at The Orchards," was the slogan he wanted everyone to remember. He established The Orchards Man of the Year award, and later The Orchards Hall of Fame. He was a people person if there ever was one, never forgetting someone's name, even if that person was a guest who had played three years earlier. Bob brought in respected assistant pros who shouldered the teaching load with the members. Bob organized events, worked with the media, and interacted with the members. While he enjoyed teaching, making people happy was even more satisfying.

In addition to the many tournaments he ran, he coordinated fun events. There was the Greenskeeper's Revenge, in which pins were placed in impossible locations on the greens, and the Italian Open, with food stations set up every few

The clubhouse originally was a carriage house. *(Michael Carroll)*

Bob giving a lesson in 2004. *(MassLive)*

holes. (This was the only time during the year Bob condoned alcohol on the course. "We could be naughty that day," he said.) Sometimes, his events were more than fun; they were personal. One year, he held the John Perotti Tournament to honor the Club's janitor. Perotti was touched that the membership had recognized him, but it was all Bob's doing.

Bob loved his job at the Club, but he was firmly committed to Mount Holyoke College as well, teaching golf to thousands of students, usually 75 in both the fall and spring semesters. He arranged classes for beginners, intermediates, and advanced players; his easy touch was welcoming to those who wanted to learn the game. He created the College's first golf team, the Lyons, leading them to many regional victories. His biggest thrill as a coach came in 1988, when the Lyons finished second in the Division III National Collegiate tournament in Iowa.

Bob was equally proud of the individual champions he helped along the way, including Mary Beth Berndt, Kathy Rourke, and Marsha Podvey. Each was named an All-American. (Anne Marie Tobin would have been an All-American, but the NCAA didn't designate women as such in the 1970s.) He accommodated individual needs and was generous with his time. "Bob was there for them," athletic director Laurie Priest would say. A case in point: Susan Bushey was a freshman when she joined the team in 1992. She had a rare inherited disorder called CMT that prevented her from controlling the muscles in one leg. At times she had difficulty

The Lyons Golf Team in 1995, captained by Susan Bushey, third from the right. *(Mount Holyoke College)*

Members of the 1988 championship team at Bob's induction into the MHC Sports Hall of Fame. *(Bob Bontempo)*

standing when she swung the club. Bob wrote a letter to the NCAA requesting that she be allowed to use a cart during her matches. They approved, and she played for four years. Bob did more than help with her game. "He was like family to me," she would say.

In 1995 the Massachusetts Women's Amateur was held at The Orchards. As luck would have it, Bob's two greatest players, Anne Marie Tobin and Kathy Rourke, faced each other in the first round. He was crushed by this pairing, which meant that one of them would lose so early in the competition. Tobin won 2 and 1, and ultimately took the tournament.

Bob remained the Lyons' coach until 1995, when family commitments became more pressing and he could no longer travel with the team. Reluctantly, he stepped down from his coaching duties, although he would continue teaching PE classes for 13 years. At the same time, Bob recognized that he could no longer put in the hours the Club needed from him, so he left the position he had held for 25 years. It was a sad moment for him and for the members, but everyone understood. It was time.

Minnie Young once said that, like her husband, Bob was devoted to the game, to The Orchards, and to the profession. No more could be asked of a club professional. Henry Bontempo would have been proud.

Audry Longo, Lyons All-American. *(Getty)*

The Lyons after 1995

Four people coached the Lyons in the years after Bontempo's retirement: Sherri McDonald (1996–1999), Theresa Collins (1999–2001), Shawn Durocher (2001–2010), and Tim Walko (2010–2020). Durocher had an especially successful tenure, grooming a couple of All-Americans, Audry Longo and Kara Solem, and taking her team to three national tournaments.

It was a tremendous surprise when, in the fall of 2020, the College decided to disband its golf team, given its past success and the fact that it played on one of the finest courses in western Massachusetts, one that it owns. Reasons cited included a lack of student interest as well as the cost of supporting the program. Students, alumnae, and their parents still have access to play The Orchards, but the physical education department no longer supports a team or provides golf instruction.

(Michael Carroll)

(Michael Carroll)

14
Anne Marie Tobin

(Mount Holyoke College Class of 1979)

ALTHOUGH SHE GREW UP in Reading, Massachusetts, Anne Marie Locke had never heard of Mount Holyoke College until one day in 1975, when her brother, a golfer who played at UMass in Amherst, told her to check out The Orchards. She immediately fell in love with the course for its beauty, and her parents loved the College for its academic rigor, so she enrolled that fall.

Bob and Tobin at '02 Orchards Women's Invitational banquet. *(Margie Riley)*

She was a walk-on, as all the players were. As a Division III school, Mount Holyoke offered no scholarships. Even though it owned a highly regarded course, golf wasn't an important sport for the College. The budget for the golf team was so small the players didn't have uniforms her first year. Uniform or not, Tobin excelled in competitions. By the time she graduated three and a half years later, she had established herself as the best golfer in the College's history. In one year alone she won the Massachusetts Intercollegiate Tournament, the New England Championship, and the Penn State Invitational, a competition for Division I schools.

Her golfing achievements continued after she left South Hadley. In time she would accumulate a record seven Mass Amateur Championship titles and be low amateur in three Mass Women's Opens, a tournament she founded. Tobin won major tournaments outside the state as well, including the New England Amateur Championship in 1990. She had been such a dominant player that in 1994 the Massachusetts Golf Association established the Anne Marie Tobin Player of the Year Award, given to the state's best amateur, which she ended up winning three times.

Tobin says that "everything good in my life has been causally connected to golf, especially being able to give back." She was president of the Women's Golf Association of Massachusetts and was the first woman to sit on the executive committee of the Massachusetts Golf Association. She was president of the Francis Ouimet Fund, which has awarded more than

Bob with Ed Twohig, Jr., head golf professional from 1995 until 2000. *(Margie Riley)*

Tobin, nee Locke, and some of her many trophies and news clippings.
(Brian Smith)

$2.5 million in scholarships to kids involved with golf, and was a cofounder of the WGAM Junior Scholarship Fund, which gives money to college-bound girls who participate in the state's junior golf program. Given all of her accolades, it came as no surprise when she was inducted into the Massachusetts Golf Hall of Fame in 2016.

Tobin gives much of the credit for her success to Mount Holyoke coach Bob Bontempo. He secured invitations for the school's Lyons to play against the best college programs in the country, an invitation extended to few Division III schools, and since the team had to pay its own way, he often used his personal funds to help them travel to these events. "I would not have become the player I did without Bob's help," she said.

CHORAGOS, THURSDAY, MAY 4, 1978 11

Sports

wins New England Golf Tournament

by Pamela Adkins

"To shoot under an 80 in those harsh wind conditions was not easy," commented Bontempo. "All the scores were high, and Anne only had a two stroke lead

The combined scores of Locke 82/79; Mary Pet McMahon 117/118 and Abby Jensen 105/89 won the team championship for Mount Holyoke College. Jensen's

second round score of 89 was her best competitive round ever. Mount Holyoke beat UMass by 22 strokes, finishing regular season competition undefeated 4-0.

May 6 and 7 the golf team travels to Pennsylvania for the Penn State Invitational. Jan Van-Muching '78 is the defending champion.

No Joy in WGAM: Mighty Tobin strikes again

By JACK O'LEARY

SOUTH HADLEY — Tara Joy opened a door on the 18th hole at the Orchards yesterday, and Anne Marie Tobin walked right in, entering the Massachusetts golf history books by securing a record fifth straight WGAM Championship.

"It doesn't get boring," said Tobin, who passed the late Floss McCloskey for consecutive wins and captured the event for the sixth time overall. "This was one of the better (final) matches I've had. I'd never been into extra holes before. I thought this might be a first."

shot on the green and 2-putted for the par and 1-up victory — the quality of golf was superior. Tobin was 1 under for the day, Joy 1 over.

For a while, it appeared Tobin would force a quick end to the proceedings. The Lynnfield attorney and wife of Bellevue G.C. head professional Jim Tobin held a 1-up edge after nine holes. After Joy won No. 1 with a par, Tobin won the second with a 3-foot birdie putt and the par-5 third with a par. Joy tied the match with a 15-foot birdie putt on No. 6, and Tobin regained the edge with a 12-foot birdie putt on No. 8.

seized the opportunity when Joy knocked her second shot on the par-4 12th into a right-side bunker.

"I knew from playing this course when I was in college (Mt. Holyoke) that that bunker is jail," Tobin said. "I hit my shot to the left side of the green and 2-putted for par."

Tobin stretched the advantage to 3-up on the par-5 13th when she put her second shot on the front fringe. She 2-putted for birdie and was 3-up with five holes to play.

Joy was quick to mount a comeback.

After Tobin missed a 7-foot birdie putt on the 15th, Joy won the par-5 16th with a tap-in birdie. Still, Tobin was 1-up with two holes to play. When she knocked her tee shot on the par-3 17th just 3 feet from the pin, and Joy's 20-foot birdie putt slipped by the hole, it appeared Tobin would retain her edge.

Instead, Tobin lost her focus and missed the 3-foot halving putt.

"I saw a little mound of sand left of my line, and all I could think of was that sand," Tobin said. "I lost it and missed the putt."

(Michael Carroll)

Part Three

The Course and Its Champions

15

1973 AIAW Tournament

"I'm more alert and attentive to everything." —*Bonnie Lauer*

IN 1973 the Association of Intercollegiate Athletics for Women held its national golf tournament at The Orchards. The AIAW had been formed a couple of years earlier because the NCAA wasn't conducting women's championships at the time. Some 103 of the top players in the nation participated, among them future professionals Hollis Stacey from Rollins, Mary Bea Porter from Arizona State, and Bonnie Lauer from Michigan State. Another talented golfer was Pat Bradley, a Westford, Massachusetts, native, who was playing for Florida International University. Ruth Elvedt, head of Mount Holyoke College's Physical Education Department, was chairman of the program, and Henry Bontempo and Andy Vitale were in the scorer's tent. One-armed golf pro Jimmy Nichols gave a clinic the day before the main event.

A player commenting on the course after a practice round observed, "It's a nice layout and tough, with lots of ditches and small greens." What she forgot to mention was how wet it was. It had been a rainy spring, and the course was not in its best condition. It was so sloppy on the 15th hole the tournament committee announced a special rule allowing players to take relief on that fairway. That didn't seem to bother Bradley, who shot a 73 the first day, beating Elisabeth Skinner's 41-year-old course record of 74. Bradley's total would have been two strokes lower, but she thought she was entitled to relief on the 13th fairway instead of the 15th. She dropped her ball into a more favorable lie when she shouldn't have; recognizing her mistake, she reported it to the officials.

The USGA official on the scene didn't know what to do. Should Bradley be disqualified for this infraction? The official called the USGA headquarters in New Jersey and explained the situation. It took them an hour and a half to determine that a two-stroke penalty and not disqualification was appropriate since she had played under the wrong rule.

Bradley's good play unraveled the next day. She was on the 12th hole when she mistakenly hit the wrong ball from the fairway. Another two-stroke penalty was added to her card. It rattled her, and she ended her round with an 85, taking herself out of contention.

Lauer was leading the tournament when play began on Friday, but this day wouldn't be as easy for her. While playing the 2nd hole, her eleventh of the day, a hard rainstorm hit.

Pat Bradley, member of the World Golf Hall of Fame. *(Shutterstock)*

It took her three putts to finish the hole, for a bogey, before everyone was called off the course. The delay was longer than most, and players threw a Frisbee behind the clubhouse to break the monotony. When play finally resumed, Lauer had difficulty finding her form and bogeyed four of the next seven holes, finishing with a 79.

Despite the rain Stacey had a great round, shooting a 73 to match the course record Bradley had set two days before, but she still trailed Lauer by three strokes when play concluded. The night before the final round Lauer was asked if the pressure of having the lead bothered her. She said it didn't, claiming, "I'm more alert and attentive to everything." She wasn't overstating, as she shot a 75 to finish the tournament three strokes lower than Stacey and take the AIAW title.

Lauer became a professional in 1975, winning two LPGA events before retiring in 1991. Hollis Stacey turned pro in 1974 and won four major championships in her 18-year career. Bradley also joined the LPGA in 1974, and would accumulate 31 victories, six of them major championships. In 1991 she was inducted into the World Golf Hall of Fame. She would return to The Orchards in 2004 as honorary host of the Women's U.S. Open.

Top: Hollis Stacey, member of the World Golf Hall of Fame. Left: Bonnie Lauer, playing for Michigan State. (*Shutterstock*)

Of the 103 participants, three played for Mount Holyoke: Judy Gaziano, Jane McDermott, and Phyllis Stever. *(Mike Riley)*

The 3rd green today. *(Dave Fraser)* Note the bottom sectional from 1921, with a central hollow and plateau to help a ball stay on the green.

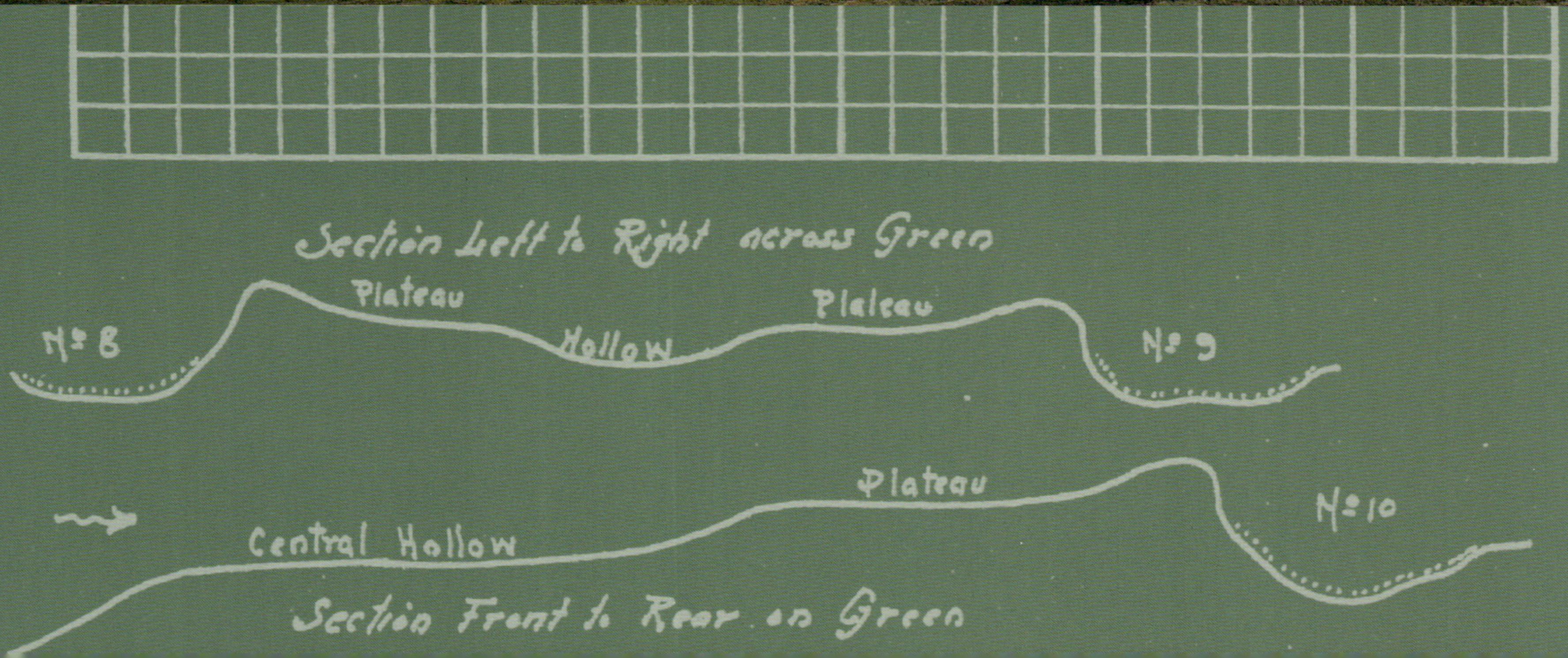

16

Changing the Design

"Stop throwing stones at the chairman of the greens committee." —*Donald Ross*

It's almost inevitable that a golf course will change over the decades, at least in America. Whether it's to keep up with the latest trends in golf course design or to remove annoying hazards, clubs invariably modify their layouts. Because The Orchards always operated on a meager budget, alterations to its course were rare. The College's primary interests lay elsewhere, so the Club was left with only enough money to maintain the property, not improve it.

Thank goodness! The changes other clubs were making to their courses created a hodgepodge in the appearance of the holes and the way they played. Members might have thought they were upgrading these courses, but they were doing just the opposite.

The only deviation from this thinking at The Orchards occurred in 1977, when it became apparent that some of the greens needed reconstructive work. As long as it was repairing these greens, the College thought it should also remodel parts of the layout, and to this end it engaged golf architect Al Zikorus. He started with the 3rd hole, an average-length par-5 whose green had a pronounced back-to-front slope, a design feature that helps prevent long fairway shots from running off the putting surface. Some members thought the hole was too easy. Zikorus raised the green and flattened it. The 8th hole was next. It had a small green, with a tier similar to the one on the 12th. Zikorus enlarged it and, as he had on the 3rd green, flattened it.

Quickly assessing the project, the College told him to stop. Not only did the greens look out of place, they were harder to play. Because of the change in the slope, balls were more likely to run off the back. Moreover, the surfaces were firmer than those of the original holes, which added to the challenge of getting an approach shot to stay on the green. Fortunately, only two greens had been renovated, and thereafter the College made no other modifications.

17
What Is a Donald Ross Course?

"His stamp as an architect was naturalism." —*Jack Nicklaus*

Greens

Ross is best known for his greens. Those who only know his work at Pinehurst No. 2 in North Carolina might think he wanted them shaped like mounds—upside-down saucer cups or tortoise shells, as they're called. But those greens are an anomaly, and they didn't start out that way. When Pinehurst No. 2 was built, its greens were relatively flat, but over the years they were heavily top-dressed with sand, and mounds began to form. After Ross's death in 1948, architects added their own touches, including shaving the grass around the greens, which accentuated their domed shape and affected the way they played.

(Michael Carroll)

Ross preferred greens that weren't domed. Chipping was important to him, so hitting a ball up these steep slopes was a challenge he probably wouldn't have liked. On most of his courses, he placed little knolls and depressions near his greens, which usually had subtle movements; if the slopes were too severe, putting would be as much luck as skill, Ross believed.

Difficulty Level

Ross built courses so everyone could enjoy the game. He allowed a player to recover from a badly struck ball; unless it landed in a water hazard, or was hit out of bounds, the penalty was often a half stroke, not a full one. There were no blind shots to contend with on his golf courses, and no bunkers in front of the greens that only the most skilled players could carry. Good shots were rewarded, but poor ones didn't detract from the fun of playing.

Layout

He built holes with greens and tees close to each other, like the courses in Scotland: there was no reason to waste valuable land. The holes were usually bold, with doglegs and generous length. The fairways zigzagged with each other

Opposite: Pinehurst No. 2, Ross's most famous design. *(Steve Szurlej)*

rather than adhering to a stiffly parallel format that would, he said, be boring. Ross usually placed his bunkers 10 to 20 yards in front of the greens, not close to them, as most architects do today. He included at least one difficult par-3 on every course, and he usually made the finishing hole a challenging par-4, unless the owner insisted on a par-5.

Beauty

Ross brought artistry to his work. He utilized the natural contours of the property he was working on, so not much soil had to be moved. His holes didn't protrude from the landscape but were woven into it. He wanted a day on the course to be "enriched by the beauty of nature," not diminished by the repurposed land.

One of the turtleback greens at Pinehurst No. 2. (*USGA*)

This cedar on the 14th hole at The Orchards, the so-called sentinel tree, was one Donald Ross would not have favored, as it blocks a shot to the green from a nearby bunker. The team that planted the pines in 1927 probably wouldn't have placed it there either. Its origin was likely a pine seed that was blown into this unpropitious spot. Once the sapling had grown, members may have believed that Ross intended it to be there. The tree was removed in the late 1990s. *(Paul Jamrog)*

The 1979 Eastern AIAW Tournament

In late September 1979, the Eastern Association of the AIAW held its annual golf championship in South Hadley. After two days of soaking rain, Penn State emerged very wet and decisively victorious. Its score of 641 was 111 strokes lower than that of Amherst, which earned second place. Penn State senior Sally Slater won the individual title, shooting rounds of 71 and 80 for a 151 total. She was the first woman to break par at The Orchards. Also on the team were Lynn Marriott, who became a renowned golf coach and author, and Jane Fitzgerald, who became a highly decorated amateur.

Penn State coach Annette Thompson with the trophy.

(Jane Fitzgerald)

(Michael Carroll)

18

Course Maintenance in the 1980s

"Let the fescues grow up and then go dormant in the summer." —*Paul Jamrog*

OPERATING UNDER a limited budget over many years eventually took its toll at The Orchards. In the early 1980s the condition of the course was deteriorating. Many bunkers needed repair, most of the greens had shrunk from their original design, and the fairways had developed turf disease owing to overwatering. Sadly, many of the older members didn't care. It didn't bother them that the course had lost its luster; they preferred to keep dues low rather than to fix the course, nor did they want their play disrupted by an active maintenance crew.

In 1984, having ignored the situation for too long, the Club finally decided to take a more proactive approach and hired thirty-year-old Paul Jamrog as superintendent. His task was daunting.

First, he eradicated the crabgrass and poa annua, which were encroaching on the fairways. He applied a herbicide, planted ryegrass to establish a base, and then overseeded it with bentgrass. He brought back the greens to their original size, which had been made smaller and rounder over time from motorized cutting machines, by reverting to old-fashioned hand mowers for better precision. He also narrowed the fairways, since the manual watering system couldn't reach all of the fairway grass. Not only was the condition of the course improving, but some of its original features, including mounds on the rehabilitated greens, were beginning to reveal themselves.

Preparing for the Girls' Junior Championship had its own set of challenges. Western Massachusetts was experiencing a drought in the early summer of 1987. For one three-week period only .2 inches of rain fell at The Orchards. Lacking an automated sprinkler system, Jamrog's team had to constantly water the course by hand, trying to keep it from burning out. In addition, the restoration work on the bunkers hadn't been completed, and a long-standing drainage problem on the 6th hole needed to be fixed. Plus, some turf disease had crept back onto the course. No one said preparing a course for a USGA championship was easy, and it was certainly not so at The Orchards that summer. But Jamrog and his team did their job well.

Next to the quality of the layout and the pedigree of its architect, a Club's most valuable asset is its greens superintendent, fancy bars and locker rooms notwithstanding.

Inset: Paul Jamrog, Bob Bontempo, and Ben Crenshaw. *(WGBY)*

19

1987 Girls' Junior Championship

"She finished the front nine on pure guts."

IT WAS A TERRIFIC HONOR when the United States Golf Association selected The Orchards to host the 1987 Girls' Junior Championship. The Club had demonstrated its bona fides by successfully hosting three qualifying tournaments for the United States Men's Amateur Championship, and golf's governing body was obviously impressed. The selection made sense. The Orchards is a fine Donald Ross layout, and because of its history, no course in America better exemplifies women's golf. It was built for a young woman who would become a champion player, and it is owned by a women's college whose students compete on its fairways. The USGA's decision merely confirmed what was already a well-earned legacy.

Mount Holyoke College hosted a welcoming dinner for the players and their families the first night of the championship. Elisabeth Skinner sat with a niece at one of the tables, still mentally sharp and spry at 95. She seldom made public appearances, however this event was different. While her golfing days were a distant memory, the welfare of The Orchards was always important to Elisabeth, so she was delighted to attend the banquet.

Tournament favorite Vicki Goetz from Georgia. ***(Getty)***

If you had to pick a favorite to win, you would be looking at three girls. Adele Moore was the runner-up at the previous year's championship at Peach Tree Golf and Country Club in California. She had won the 1986 Girls' Junior PGA Championship, the only other national tournament at the time. Vicki Goetze was another standout golfer. Just fourteen, she won the Girls' PGA earlier in 1987 and competed in the Women's Open in July. And there was a 17-year-old from Florida who checked all the boxes. She made it to the finals at the 1987 Girls' PGA, to the third round at Peach Tree, and for two years she won all her state's junior events. So Michelle McGann's name was on the list as well.

Some 209 girls entered the competition, and after qualifying rounds 150 made it to South Hadley. The format would be two rounds of medal, or stroke, play. The best 64 players would compete in single elimination match play, and after six rounds the best female junior golfer in the world would be declared.

Most of the girls were accompanied by their parents, staying at one of the nearby inns. But not all parents made the trip. In keeping with junior golf tradition, some players stayed with local families, who gladly fed them, provided a

Top: Elisabeth with Peggy Armistead, a niece, at the welcoming dinner. *(Bill Armistead)* **Above: Michelle McGann on the left and Lynn Mikulas in the final round.** *(USGA)*

comfortable bed, and cheered them on each day. About 40 players were hosted by local families that week. One was Goetze, up from Hull, Georgia. She spent the week with the Orlen family of South Hadley. As often happens, a close bond was formed, and they kept in touch for many years.

All the favorites played well on the first day, with McGann carding an impressive 73. If she had managed a similar round on Tuesday she would certainly have had a spot in match play. But Tuesday's round wasn't similar to Monday's. Not in the least. A Type 1 diabetic, McGann relied on injections and frequent nourishment to manage her condition. She had done it well in the past, but on the front nine of the second round her regimen failed her. She became dizzy, and her legs were weakening. Her blood sugar was low, and she was struggling to make it to the turn. After nine holes her scorecard read 45, nine over par. Her tournament was about to slip away. But the bananas she finally received on the 10th and 13th tees did wonders. McGann scored a 33 on the back nine for a miraculous 78. "She finished the front nine on pure guts," her father, Bucky, would say. Her 151 total for the two rounds tied Brandie Burton and Lisa Brandetsas for the medalist title.

There was a poignant moment on the 18th green on Wednesday when Goetze faced Terri Thompson, also from Georgia. They were friends, having played together on the junior circuit, and Goetze made the 1,000-mile trip to South Hadley with the Thompsons. As occasionally happens in tennis and match play golf, good friends meet early in the draw, and unfortunately, these two had to face each other in the second round. The match went to the final hole, which Goetze won. They hugged. The tournament was over too quickly for Thompson, who had made it to the fourth round the year

In Appreciation of the Hospitality of

The Orchards Golf Course

1987 United States Girls' Junior Championship

Conducted by the United States Golf Association

The Players

Claudia Lyland
Tracy Little
Kim Tyrer
Tina Trimble
Nasim Kronske
Laura Saiki
Jennifer Lasky
Lisa Weissmueller
Dawn Chmaousky
Valerie Stull
Stephanie Martin
Sue Veasey
Tonya Blosser
Tonya Sice
Tina Paternostro
Stephanie Comstock
Teri Thompson
Vicki Goetze
Kim Byham
Ami Schonauer
Lauren Stivers
Christina Dacri
Dana Arnold
Donna Lippstreu
Tricia Allen
Maria Castellucci
Nicole Kochaphum
Nicole Horner
Lisa Brandetsas
Kelly Kluska
Candy Morgan
Carrie Kotoduvodo
Lorinda Garner
Kimberly Steffensen
Mandy Stahlman
Sharon Roth
Adele Moore
Kristie M. Kakugawa

Mary Jo Rollins
Samantha Patel
Michele Robinson
Tami Proctor
Emma Rundle
Cappy Mack
Lucia Kong
Heather Anne Lee
Jennifer Holt
Alyssa Ramlein
Jodie Ladone
Kristin Clark
Alison Colyer
Debbie Donger
Stacy Linn
Pepe Wagner
Angie Mills
Anne Childress
Amy McDonald
Maggy Tell
Susan Poland
Debbie Minter
Alisha Swanson
Susie Klein
Camille Codden
Tori Stinson
Jennifer Shillington
Christy Erb
Rachel McGladery
Julie Shephard
Michelle Malkin
Susan McCarthy
Debbie Parks
Starla Yamada
Tracy Duhre
Lynne Mikulas
Vivian Overturf

Jessica T. Wood
Brandie Burton
Elizabeth Bowman
Cathy Cordage
Michelle Schneider
Shannon L. Clark
Heidi Voorhess
Linda Chen
Melissa Goble
Cheryl Duff
Marie J. Rouleau
Kim Brozek
Tami Dwyer
Lisa LaBelle
Ginger Howe
Laura Myers
Anna Emmons
Jennifer Lynn Ausland
Leigh Dickey
Erica Zonder
Barbara Morace
Kimberly Cayce
Meredith Lousse
Erin Johnson
Sandy Hemby
Beth Manczak
Kristin Ingram
Erin Haney
Vicki Casey
Julie Purvey
Cindi Schaaf
Julie M. Batterson
Tracy Hanson
Shelley Triplett
Lori Anne Graban
Audrey Wooding
Stephanie Davis

Marian Sisson
Debbie Eckroth
Lynette Windsor
Becky Wilson
Tracy Cone
Jane Henry
Nikki Valentine
Leslie Green
Mary Dunne
Trisha Corace
Vicki Schocki
Stacy Jo Smith
Justina Hopkins
Kim Augusta
Nicole Forthe
Meghan Hannafin
Meg Young
Maggie Herold
Susan Slaughter
Amy Conners
Brigitte Jagemann
Bronwyn Burke
Michelle McGann
Angie Wilson
Krista Bantenfeldt
Kris Leighton
Laura Blegne
Wendy Bigler
Chris Wollack
Coley Jordan
Cindi Isaac
Jodi Zwemke
Barbara L. Blackwell
LeRee Pearl Luzy
Marti Longoria
Jody-Marie Cosgrove
Annette Kealoha
Allyson Green

Official Match Play Score Card
39th United States
Girls' Junior Championship®
Conducted by the United States Golf Association

The Orchards Golf Course
Mount Holyoke College
South Hadley, Massachusetts
August 10-15, 1987

Girls' Junior

U.S. Girls' Junior Championship
At Orchards Golf Course
South Hadley
Yesterday's Results

Quarterfinals
Elizabeth Bowman, Bonita, Calif., def. Tonya Gill, Stone Mountain, Ga., 4 and 3
Lynne Mikulas, La Mesa, Cali... def. Dana A...

USGA
U.S. GIRLS' JU...OR
AUGUST 10-15
THE ORCHARDS GOLF COURSE/SC...ETTS

Girls' Junior
Trio shares medal

By STEVE KELLY
SOUTH HADLEY — Michelle McGann needed a little food — and an 18th hole bir...

Above: Elisabeth greeting McGann on the first tee. *(Bill Armistead)*

Left: McGann with the Vare Trophy. *(USGA)*

before. She would watch her friend continue in the championship before they made the long trip back to Georgia.

The favorites advanced through the first three rounds. In the fourth round, McGann squared off against Adele Moore, and a tight duel was anticipated. Leaning on her superior length off the tee, McGann defeated her, 3 and 2. While not a rout, it was an impressive win, as she convincingly knocked off the prior year's runner-up.

That afternoon McGann played her fifth match against Goetze. Someone called it a clash of titans, although David versus Goliath may have been more appropriate, as McGann stood half a foot taller than her opponent. McGann could hit the ball a long way, but her shots weren't always straight. Goetze didn't drive her ball far, but it always landed in the fairway. Two great players with two different games. But it wasn't the close battle everyone had expected, as Goetze didn't win a hole the entire match, losing 8 and 6. It was a stunning victory for McGann; something very special was happening. On Saturday she would face Lynn Mikulas from La Mesa, California, to determine the champion.

At Bob Bontempo's invitation, Elisabeth Skinner arrived at the circle around the putting green to greet the finalists as they were about to tee off. From the window of the car, she shook hands with McGann and Mikulas, wishing them luck.

Incredibly, McGann was 6 up after the first seven holes. Like most of her other matches, this one was almost too easy, although she would never say that. That wasn't her personality. Besides, match play can turn quickly, as all the players knew. Going into the final hole of the match, McGann had nine pars, one birdie, one bogey, and one conceded hole before she finished off Mikulas with a birdie on the 13th for a 7 and 5 victory. And the trophy.

In her six rounds, McGann needed only 88 holes to complete her matches. It was the third fewest in Girls' Junior Championship history, with none of her matches reaching the 17th hole. Given the strength of the field, it was a tour de force performance few had predicted.

With her parents and little brother in attendance, McGann cried at the trophy presentation. Despite the drubbing she took, Mikulas said she was happy for McGann: "She's a really nice person, and I like her a lot." Teenagers learn many things from golf, including how to lose with grace.

Goetze would continue her stellar amateur career. In 1988 and 1990 she was named Player of the Year by the Junior Golf Association, and at 16 she won the U.S. Women's Amateur. Six girls from the tournament, including McGann and Goetze, would become professionals.

McGann's victory was the finale of her amateur playing days. In 1987, *Golf Digest* and *Golf Magazine* named her Amateur of the Year. Twenty-five years later, the Girls' Junior Championship remained an important moment in her life. "I think about it all the time," she said. "Your name is on the [Vare] trophy. It's in Far Hills, New Jersey. It's so special."

As were those six remarkable days in August 1987.

ELISABETH SKINNER
THE FIRST LADY OF GOLF
AT THE ORCHARDS

20

Elisabeth's Last Bow

"She was delightful, cordial, and very generous." —Marion Kohler

After Joseph's death, in 1946, Elisabeth remained in the mansion. He had left the estate to Mount Holyoke College with the understanding that she could live there the rest of her life. While Joseph lived lavishly, with a Rolls-Royce and a chauffeur, Elisabeth lived modestly among the beautiful items he had left in the house, which was filled with oil paintings, Tiffany lamps, and fine American furniture.

Elisabeth rarely spoke of her golf achievements. Whenever asked, she'd say, "Well, I guess I was pretty good, but that was a long time ago," and that would be it. She preferred to inquire about the goings-on of others rather than to talk about herself.

Minnie Young said of Elisabeth, "She was very nice, but you couldn't get close to her." Indeed, Elisabeth was reserved, yet her manner toward others wasn't the result of any discourtesy. She enjoyed warm, private conversations with people but eschewed small talk, and she rarely attended large social gatherings. She had friends in the community, formed either through a mutual interest, such as cards, or because she was a thoughtful neighbor. Social status never played a role in those she befriended. As long-time friend William Dwight pointed out, "Elisabeth could have been one of those Kipling characters who could 'Walk with the mighty and keep the common folk.' "

Marion Kohler was a neighbor who visited Elisabeth every day, and they'd chat about politics and the news. "She was a dear," she said of her friend. Jimmy Young's son Bill remembers the time he was sick as a child when she brought him a present to cheer him up. "She was very kind to me and my family," he said. Elisabeth enjoyed children. At Halloween, her maid would invite trick-or-treaters into the mansion, and Elisabeth would talk to them for a few minutes, asking about their families. Carl Chaffee was 10 years old when he rang the doorbell one Halloween, and he was enthralled by what he saw in the home. He came back to visit many times, and she gave

Apple tree on the 4th hole with a marker honoring Elisabeth. *(Michael Carroll)*

him the run of the house, allowing him to explore the beautiful rooms and play games in the basement. They remained friends for 15 years. All who knew Elisabeth enjoyed her pleasant demeanor and appreciated her many acts of kindness. She was reserved but insightful, modest despite having much to be immodest about. That was her way.

In her later years Elisabeth spent most of her time in one of the sitting rooms, with a television set that was usually tuned to golf. She enjoyed watching Seve Ballesteros, her favorite player. When Elisabeth played, her drives usually split the fairways, while Ballesteros could seldom find one; but he always found a way to win, and that's what she liked about him.

Five weeks after the 1987 Girls' Championship came to a close, Elisabeth passed away. The College lowered its flag to half-staff, and a memorial note was placed at the base of the flagpole. She was inducted into the Western Massachusetts Golf Hall of Fame in memoriam in 2015.

Whenever asked, Elisabeth would say that her father had built The Orchards because he wanted a place for the townspeople to play. But everyone knew he had built it for her.

"Elisabeth could 'Walk with the mightly and keep the common folk.'" —*William Dwight*

Front stairway of Elisabeth's home; Elisabeth with Margaret Selig, a great-niece, and two rooms in the mansion. *(Richard Selig)*

Joseph and Elisabeth invited community members into their home to support "Bundles for Britain" when Laurence Olivier visited in 1941.
(Richard Selig)

(Michael Carroll)

Part Four
A Change and an Open

MARY LYON HALL

21

The College's Role as Overseer

"We have one of the top golf courses and . . . best colleges for women." —*Laurie Priest*

FROM THE TIME Mount Holyoke took ownership of The Orchards, in 1941, the College controlled everything associated with the golf course. It determined how much money should be spent each year, where it would go, and the amount of revenue needed to offset expenses.

In the early 1970s the College agreed to bring the membership into the decision-making process, something the members had requested for many years. The College established a Board of Directors, and it held the majority of the seats, so it would have control of the more important matters. However, the members got the flexibility in the day-to-day decisions they wanted. The arrangement worked well.

Over the ensuing decades, whenever capital improvements were needed, the College loaned the necessary funds, providing extended repayment terms at low interest rates. In 1997 a number of structural repairs to the course were required as well as a new maintenance facility, and the board wanted a long-term master plan for The Orchards. A $1.5 million loan was made, which was far greater than previous investments.

(Dave Fraser)

It was around this time that the College's Board of Directors conducted a complete review of its real estate holdings. A subcommittee proposed that the College should be earning a 10 percent return on any asset it owned that wasn't used for educational purposes, such as rental housing, the local Village Commons retail operation, and The Orchards. An appraiser was hired, who placed a $4.4 million value on the golf course. The College's relationship with the Club's membership had been good over the years, but with the increasing financial outlays

(Hans Teensma)

Wayne Gass from Mount Holyoke, left, with Bob Bontempo and Fred Lane, president of the Club.

and the growing burden of watching over its investment, perhaps it was time for another entity to manage the property.

The coincidence of the high appraisal and the desire to disengage made the College's decision easy. It sent out a request for proposal to some 40 golf management companies, including the Club's board, to lease and operate The Orchards. Two offers were received; one from the Arnold Palmer Golf Management Company of Dallas, Texas, the other from the Club. Palmer would pay $400,000 per year to lease the property, while the Club proposed $265,000. Members of the Club felt that Palmer's bid was unrealistic: it would be impossible for the company to provide an acceptable level of course conditions and make other improvements, yet still make a profit. However, the College saw it differently, and it selected Palmer to manage The Orchards under a 25-year lease, beginning on January 1, 2000.

(Opposite clockwise: Michael Carroll, Phil Schermeister, Massachusetts Office of Travel and Tourism)

22

The Palmer Group

"Manzi was a magician." —*USGA Director Tom Meeks*

On January 1, 2000, Mount Holyoke entered into a 25-year lease with The Palmer Group. Its strategy was to upgrade The Orchards and turn it into a first-rate facility that would draw members from beyond the immediate area, such as from Boston and Hartford. In addition to making improvements to the golf course, it totally revised the existing clubhouse, with new locker rooms and a refashioned dining area.

Palmer planned to raise the Club's dues to get a return on its investment, expecting that a small number of members would leave, but they would be replaced by wealthier members who could afford the higher payments. Palmer's timing seemed good. Golf was in another of its boom phases in the 1990s. People had become enamored with Tiger Woods, and there were plenty of newcomers to the sport. The economy and the stock market were soaring, so people had disposable cash to invest in a round of golf, if not a membership. The town of South Hadley recognized this trend, and it opened its own course, The Ledges, in 2001.

(Hans Teensma)

However, by 2002 cracks were beginning to form in the golfing landscape. The stock market had crashed, and people weren't spending money as freely as they had, and this included golf. When the USGA announced in April 2002 that it was moving the Women's Open to The Orchards in 2004, Palmer saw a tremendous opportunity to boost its membership ranks. The Orchards would no longer be a hidden gem, as golfers would witness a USGA championship on national television, contested on a Donald Ross course in South Hadley.

To fulfill these dreams, Palmer needed to do a lot of work to prepare the course for the Open and the television audience. Superintendent Matt Manzi had a difficult task in the spring of 2004. He had just been brought

Scenes from the mid-1990s. *(Margie Riley)*

over from another Palmer golf course after The Orchards' previous superintendent resigned. He was still learning the idiosyncrasies of the property as he was preparing for the championship. It had been a tough winter in western Massachusetts, and the effects of the many subzero days were apparent at the course. The greens had severe ice damage, and the fairways suffered from a delay in the growing season. Moreover, there was a lot of logistical work to be done. Everyone was concerned that The Orchards wouldn't be ready in just three short months.

With the help of the USGA's agronomy team, Manzi and his crew worked tirelessly to get the course in shape. The USGA spent more time and money preparing for this tournament than it did for any of its other championship venues that year. The partnership worked. By the time the first ball was struck, the course was nearly perfect. Twice during the Open, on national TV, USGA Director Tom Meeks called Manzi "a magician."

Once again, it took a pending USGA championship to bring out the very best from the Club's superintendent and his crew.

Mount Holyoke College students have always had access to the course.
(Michael Carroll)

2004 U.S. Women's Open
Championship
Orchards Golf Club at Mount Holyoke College
June 28 - July 4 • South Hadley, Mass.
ORCHARDS
MEMBER
2004 U.S. WOMEN'S OPEN
THE ORCHARDS
SUNDAY
DAILY TICKET
July 4, 2004
Ticket must be displayed at all times.
NO REFUNDS OR EXCHANGES. NO CELL PHONES.
NO CAMERAS. NO COOLERS. NO CHAIRS WITH ARMS.
CONDUCTED BY THE UNITED STATES GOLF ASSOCIATION
00253
USGA
OPEN
THE ORCHARDS

23

2004 Women's U.S. Open

"It's such a timeless place."

California's Lake Merced Golf Club was supposed to host the Women's Open Championship in 2003. But the USGA determined that a large construction project it was planning would cause logistical problems for the event, so it had to look elsewhere. Pumpkin Ridge, in Oregon, which was slated for the tournament in 2004, agreed to move to 2003. That left the USGA scrambling for a site for 2004.

Joan Fay, wife of USGA executive director David Fay, had just attended an alumnae golf tournament at Mount Holyoke, and Laurie Priest, its head of athletics, mentioned how much the College would love to host another U.S. Girls' Junior Championship. When Joan learned of the USGA's concerns about Lake Merced, she suggested to her husband that The Orchards would fill this spot nicely. David called the president of the Massachusetts Golf Association for some insights into the course. Ten days after he learned that The Orchards was not simply a good course, but a great course, he called Priest. She was stunned to hear him say that the USGA didn't want to bring the girls back to South Hadley, it wanted to bring the women—this time for the U.S. Open in 2004.

The Contenders

One hundred fifty-six of the world's best women golfers participated, including 16 amateurs. Some were veterans hoping to put together four more days of perfect golf before exiting the sport, but most were professionals who had never won a major tournament.

Annika Sorenstam had seven major trophies in her display case, and she had already been inducted into the World Golf Hall of Fame. Soft-spoken, the 33-year-old from Sweden appeared shy at times, but she was fiercely competitive.

USGA

UNITED STATES GOLF ASSOCIATION 1894

The Women's Committee
of the
United States Golf Association
cordially invites you to attend a
Championship Celebration Reception
immediately following the
Prize Presentation Ceremony

Sunday, July 4, 2004
Orchards Golf Club

Attire: come as you are from the course

R.S.V.P. by June 4

Clockwise from top left: Michelle Wie *(Alamy)*; **Brittany Lincicome** *(USGA)*; **Annika Sorenstam.** *(Alamy)*

She was the one to beat, and everyone knew it. However, a 14-year-old phenom from Hawaii was inching into the spotlight. Michelle Wie was a prodigy of the first order. She was six feet tall, slim, and athletic. She had won the U.S. Public Links at age 13, a remarkable feat. The USGA extended an invitation for her to bypass a qualifying tournament to play the '04 Open. She was the first amateur to receive this exemption, but nobody was complaining. While Wie was unlikely to take the trophy, a throng of people, including parents with daughters in tow, turned out to watch her play. She could hit 290-yard drives. Might she overpower the course?

July 1, Play Commences

It rained the first day—not of biblical proportions, but hard enough for water to pool on some greens. Play was suspended. Twice. Seventy-five players, including Sorenstam, would have to wait until the following morning to complete their rounds. Unlike most competitors, who were staying at one of the hotels in Springfield, Sorenstam was encamped at a house she'd rented on the 13th fairway, the highest point on the course. That night a thunderstorm woke her. "I didn't get a lot of sleep," she would say. She was up at 4:30 to meet a 7:00 start time to finish three holes. She double-bogeyed her first hole, the difficult 16th, and completed her first round at 71, even par. Wie had a 71 as well.

It was another amateur, a 19-year-old from St. Petersburg, Florida, who took the lead on the first day. Qualifier Brittany Lincicome made an eagle from under the trees on hole 15 en route to a stellar five-under-par round. She and her caddying father cried as they walked up to the 15th green. The moment exemplified one of the great thrills of Open golf when, on rare occasions, an amateur fires a miraculous round to lead the championship. While it's exciting, the extraordinary play is often fleeting. Even pros find it difficult to follow up a spectacular round with another the next day. So it wasn't surprising when Lincicome shot a 77 on day 2 and disappeared from the leaderboard. Jennifer Rosales, the first woman from the Philippines to win an LPGA event, posted a 67 to take a one-stroke lead on day 2, and on day 3 she carded a 69. Heading into the final round, she was three shots ahead of Sorenstam, Kelly Robbins, and veteran Meg Mallon.

"I gave it my all." —Annika Sorenstam

Mallon was out to prove she wasn't too old to compete, even though her only Open victory had come 13 years earlier. Sunday started well for her. After parring the first two holes, she birdied the par-5 3rd, then sank an improbable 54-foot curling downhill putt for birdie on the steeply sloped 4th green. She bowed and laughed, seemingly embarrassed by her good fortune. That was Mallon's demeanor, fun and breezy, which was quite the opposite of Sorenstam's quiet, steely grit. At the moment, the extrovert was winning. With Rosales and Robbins struggling, the tournament was coming down to Sorenstam and Mallon.

Many of Mallon's family were in the crowd, and on this day they had plenty of opportunities to cheer. She birdied 9, 11, 12, and 14. On 15, a wayward approach shot followed

In Appreciation of the Hospitality of

Orchards Golf Club

2004 United States Women's Open Championship

Conducted by the United States Golf Association

The Players

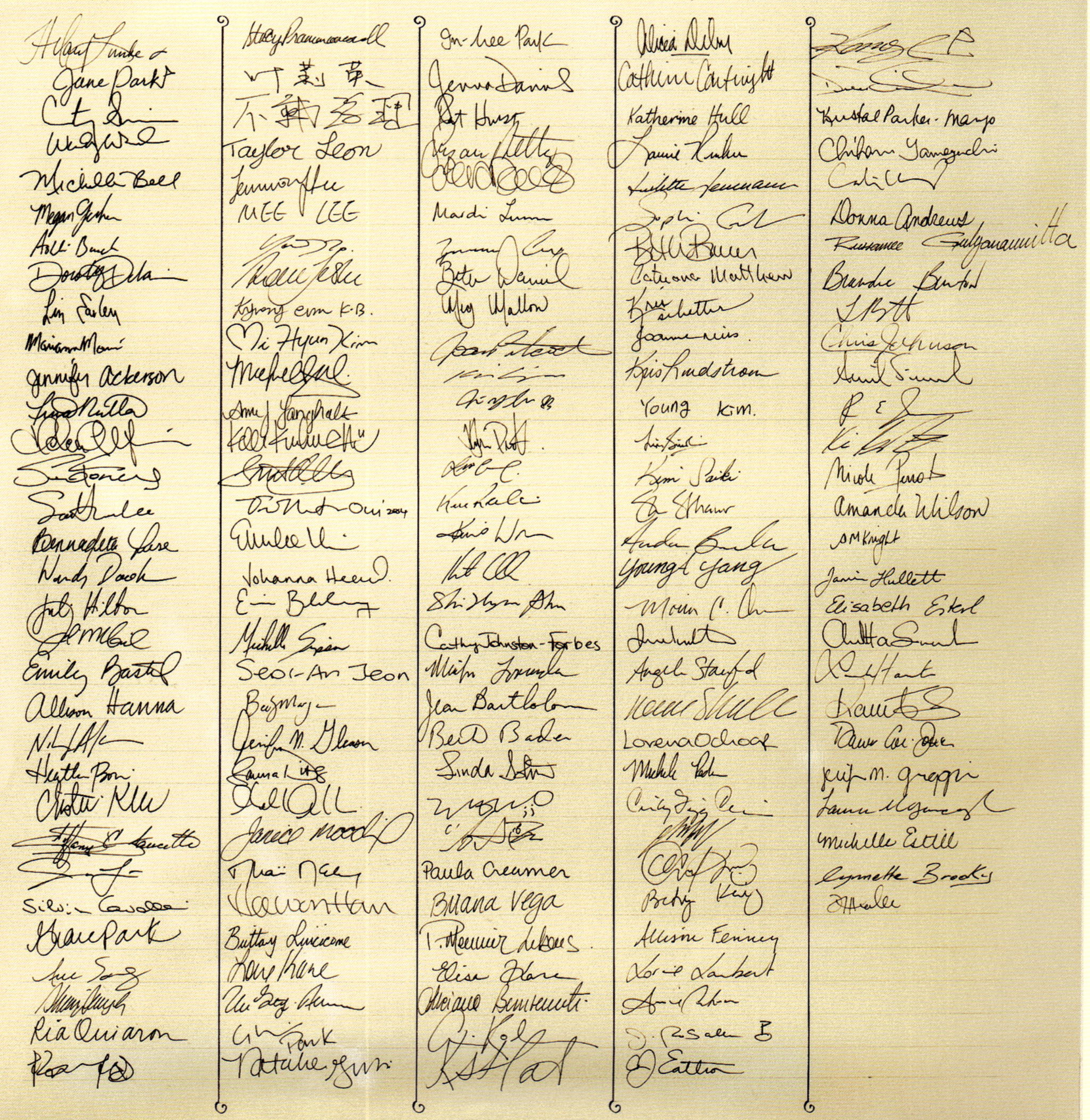

Sorenstam walking up the 18th fairway on Sunday. *(USGA)*

by a muffed chip left her in the fringe of the green. Facing a long putt for par, her magical putter saved her once again. The crowd erupted when the ball dropped into the hole, and Mallon's apologetic smile flashed anew. Two pars followed. Standing on the 18th tee, she was 10 under par.

But Sorenstam was a fighter. Playing ahead of Mallon, she birdied 10, 13, and 17. On 18 she made another putt for birdie, pumping her fist in celebration. She finished the tournament 8 under par, two shots behind Mallon. For Sorenstam to earn a tie and a playoff, Mallon would have to double-bogey the last hole. She would have to wait 10 minutes for the final verdict.

The 18th at The Orchards is one of its most challenging holes, an uphill par-4 measuring 412 yards. For the week, it was playing almost a half stroke over par. Mallon's drive found the fairway, and her approach shot landed on the left side of the green. Fortunately for her, the ball settled below the incline that traverses it, leaving her with a level putt. She had been putting well all day, so the outcome wasn't in doubt. She took two putts to make par, clinching the championship by two strokes over Sorenstam. Mallon needed only 24 putts to complete her round that day. Her 65 set a women's record at The Orchards, and it was the lowest final round recorded by a champion at an Open. After the round she told the press corps how much she loved the untouched Ross layout, noting "It's such a timeless place."

Sorenstam confessed that she was disappointed in the final result, but remarked that she would get over it. "I gave it my all," she said. As for the wunderkind from Hawaii, Wie finished the tournament at one over par, tied with Paula Creamer for low amateur honors. More would be heard from them.

The 2004 Open was an overwhelming success. Commentators spoke glowingly of The Orchards and its history, and the television audience enjoyed a thrilling event. The championship had a Women's Open record turnout of 118,458 fans, and, thanks to the support of the entire Mount Holyoke College community, there were 2,600 volunteers, who did everything from marshalling the crowds to running the scoreboard. Gratifyingly, the players gave favorable reviews of the golf course. But would the Goodyear blimp ever come back to The Orchards?

The clubhouse is small, practice areas are cramped, and players had to drive to Springfield to find the accommodations they desired. Meanwhile, some of America's most hallowed venues were eyeing the event. The women would travel to historic Newport Country Club in 2006, and Oakmont, which had already hosted the Women's Open in 1992, invited them back in 2010. It would be difficult to compete with these and other thoroughbreds in the future.

Barring another moment of serendipity, 2004 will probably be The Orchards' only U.S. Open, and that will be fine. Tournament golf doesn't allow mulligans, and The Orchards didn't need one. It was beautifully presented for the championship, and it survived the downpour. The course revealed itself to be a challenging but fair layout for the world's best players. If you're given an opportunity in life to try something extraordinary and you do it well, you don't need to do it again. By all accounts, the tournament that had miraculously landed in the lap of The Orchards had gone well. Very well.

Meg Mallon with the Semple Trophy. *(USGA)*

FINAL SCORES
Meg Mallon–10
Annika Sorenstam–8
Kelly Robbins–6
Jennifer Rosales–3
Michele Redman–2
Candie Kung–2

59TH U.S. WOMEN'S OPEN CHAMPIONSHIP
MALLON
TODAY THRU 17 TOTAL
6 MALLON 10
4 ROSALES 3

24

After the Open

"This is golf in its purest form." —*Chris Tallman*

As SUCCESSFUL as the Open had been, the nationally televised event didn't attract the hordes of new members The Palmer Group had hoped for. Fallout from the punctured dotcom bubble continued to plague the golf industry. People weren't getting into the game, they were leaving it.

Because it was losing money, Palmer let go some of the men who took care of the course and the lack of attention showed. What the members had predicted when it met with the College seven years earlier had come true. It wasn't long before Palmer transferred its lease rights and obligations to Century Golf, another management company. But it, too, struggled to make a profit.

General Manager Chris Tallman.
(Dave Fraser)

In 2016, CBIGG, a golf course management firm based in Sugar Land, Texas, acquired the lease from Century, bringing a commitment to The Orchards that previous managers had lacked. The following year, Dave Parson moved up from Rye, New York, where he was an assistant course superintendent at the Apawamis Club, to be the head superintendent. His expertise in tending to other courses quickly became apparent. Parson won the approval from local environmental groups to start a much-needed tree removal project, he fixed the many bunkers that needed repair, and brought the greens back to their original shape. His dedication to the job was inspiring, and a picture of him working in darkness circulated through the clubhouse. Members were smiling once again.

In 2019 Chris Tallman became general manager. Having grown up in South Hadley, he knew the course well. He brought to his job a positive attitude, which was refreshing. People were joining the Club again, in part because Covid had shut down most alternative forms of recreation, but also because they liked what they were seeing. The Orchards was starting to look the way it had on television during the Open.

Positive change was occurring at the Club, a revival members had been waiting for.

(Michael Carroll)

(Michael Carroll)

Part Five
People

25

Playing with the Pros

"Hit it hard. It will land somewhere." —*Mark Calcavecchia*

Before the Satellite Tour began in 1990, many golf professionals earned their living by playing small tournaments around the country, hoping someday they would qualify for the PGA Tour. From 1979 until 1999, The Orchards had a pro-am run by Club member Bill Dupont and head professional Bob Bontempo. The event paired 40 professionals with local amateurs, often Club members, for a two-day tournament. In 1979 the cost for amateurs to participate was $75. Many top players came to the event, including eventual British Open champion Mark Calcavecchia, PGA champion Jeff Sluman, Ken Green, and Jim Chancey. One year, Chancey shot a 62, setting the course record. It was an important event for the community that attracted many local sponsors, volunteers, and plenty of fans. It was fun.

The pro-am was meant to showcase The Orchards, but it was also used to raise money for the Club. After the purse was divided with the pros and all expenses were paid, the Club usually netted about $10,000. That might have been peanuts for some clubs, but it was an important source of revenue for The Orchards. The annual pro-am returned to The Orchards in 2019, and, unlike the previous iteration, women were welcome to join. This event is smaller than the original one, with between 15 and 18 professionals usually appearing. Prominent players such as Scott Berliner, Fran Marrello, and James Hervol have participated, and as before, it's fun. But now the net proceeds don't go back to the Club; they go to a local charity. From 2019 to 2021 the Club donated more than $10,000 to Neighbors Helping Neighbors, a food pantry in South Hadley.

General manager Chris Tallman brought the prestigious Western Mass Open to The Orchards in 2019. About 40 professionals have been joining 60 amateurs each year to compete for prizes. Tim Umphrey, a PGA professional, won in 2021 with a 5-under-par round of 66. Tallman competed, but he finished seven strokes behind. It isn't easy playing well in a tournament you're running.

Neighbors Helping Neighbors, Inc.

Clockwise from the top left: Jeff Sluman *(Alamy)*; **Tim Umphrey and Cameron Moniz** *(Staff of The Orchards)*; **Mark Calcavecchia, Raymond Floyd, and Ken Green.** *(Alamy)*

Course marks go tumbling

South Hadley woman shines at Longmeadow CC

It's been a banner year for local women in course record-setting circles. Bonnie Catto of South Hadley was the latest record breaker when she fired a 5-under-par 67 from the red tees Tuesday at Longmeadow Country Club.

Tee talk

Catto captures WMass Amate

Pittsfield at Watertown

$5,025.

The Orchards' Catto state publinx champ

BOSTON — Alistair Catto of The Orchards outlasted Bob Avellino of Far Corner Golf Club, Boxford, in a three-hole sudden-death playoff yesterday to win the Massachusetts Golf Association's state public links championship at George Wright Golf Course.

Catto and Avellino had identical rounds of 73-72 for a 5-over-par total of 145, one shot ahead of The Orchards' Dean Godek, who finished third at 72-74-146.

The MGA picked the first, eighth and ninth holes for the playoff.

The rivals tied the first two in par with Catto getting a two-putt par on the long par-four ninth for the victory when Avellino was unable to get it up-and-down from just off the green.

... one of my happiest days in ... golf title,"

26

Alistair and Bonnie Catto

". . . but to get two holes-in-one in eight days?" —*Alistair Catto*

If the Club had a Lifetime Achievement for Couples award, Bonnie and Alistair Catto would have won it. Between them, they won 17 Club Championships. Some people called Alistair quirky, probably because of the clothes he favored, but everyone called him an excellent golfer. Bonnie was, too. Alistair didn't start playing the game until he was 26 years old, but within four years he was shooting in the sixties. From 1985 to 2000 he was the best amateur in western Massachusetts, winning almost every tournament he entered. He often traveled out of the state to compete, usually for a USGA event. In 1990 he qualified for the U.S. Amateur at Cherry Hills.

Alistair could easily be considered the Club's international ambassador, with Scotland and his native England his favorite destinations. He competed in the British Amateur and the St. Andrews Links Trophy match, to name only two. The list is too long. He was always traveling, often with Bonnie as his caddy. In 1992 alone, Alistair played in two championships in Great Britain, two USGA events, and five tournaments in New England. Over his career, he racked up nine holes-in-one, which included three at The Orchards. One was on the difficult 7th hole.

Bonnie still carries a 7.5 handicap, but it was lower when she competed. She won local tournaments and played in many regional competitions, including the New England Amateur and the Women's Eastern Amateur. One year she was semifinalist in the MGA's Amateur Match Play Championship. She also played in USGA events. In 1995 she was the medalist in qualifying for the U.S. Public Links, and later she played in two Senior Women's U. S. Amateur Championships. Her best score at The Orchards was 71, but that didn't compare to the 67 she shot at Longmeadow one day, when it was hosting the state's stroke play tournament.

In 2008 Alistair was inducted into the Western Massachusetts Hall of Fame; Bonnie followed suit seven years later. No other couple has achieved that distinction.

Bonnie with brother-in-law Colin Catto and Ray Roberts. ***(Alistair Catto)***

19
LUDLOW
21

27

Membership

"The Club is in my heart."

PEOPLE JOIN CLUBS for different reasons: tennis courts, a swimming pool, fine dining, and socializing with one's peers all factor into the decision. Another reason is golf. Men, especially, want a place to play and entertain. The Orchards offers golf, and only golf. It is the finest course in the area, so serious golfers gravitate to Silverwood Terrace, even if another club might offer more amenities. They join because the Club is straightforward and unostentatious. While the course is hard, the atmosphere is easy; some join for the camaraderie alone. Members don't care that the clubhouse is small and unadorned, and the cuisine doesn't boast a Michelin star. Let them go to The Country Club in Brookline for that. It's cozy and inviting at The Orchards, and that's why they like it.

There are doctors, lawyers, and dentists in the Club's ranks, people who can afford to belong to a couple of clubs. And some do. But most are small-business owners, teachers, or administrators, and many are retired. They're from the South Hadley area, a prosperous but not wealthy community, so they need to watch what they spend. As one would expect, dues have risen dramatically over the years. In 1970 a member paid only $275 per year. Today it costs about $5,000, which is a huge increase from the pre-Palmer days, but it's still far less than what other clubs with Ross layouts charge. Members don't have to pay for any frills at The Orchards.

The Club has always had female members. Women were welcome to join, whether as a member of a family or independently. They sat on the board and helped organize events, and the men treated them as a part of the golfing community. Women created their own tournaments, including the September Cup, an annual competition against Ludlow Country Club. Almost every female member will tell you she loves The Orchards, despite the fact that some find it very challenging to play the course. The women's course rating of 73.2 and a slope of 132 are among the highest in the area. Heavy rainfall in 2021 added to the difficulty as the rough grew more quickly than normal. To keep it at its desired height of two inches, the crew will probably need to take an extra pass over it each week. That, and less rain in 2022, should make the course a little easier to play in its centennial year.

Clockwise from top left: Competitors for the annual September Cup ***(Margie Riley)*****;**
Nobue Yamashita, frequent 9-Hole champion ***(Margie Riley)*****; lunch on the porch after a round.** ***(Dave Fraser)***

Members of the Pine Tree Gang. *(Margie Riley)*

A club isn't defined only by its members but also by the groups within it. In the fifties, The Orchards had the Pallbearers' Club, formed by member Artie Lepine, who, not according to plan, found himself driving the hearse at his grandfather's funeral. Despite the solemn occasion, everyone laughed at the sight, and a club was formed to mark the occasion. It played only twice a year, but it was a major event, drawing prominent sportsmen from around the area. Starting with six members, the club grew to 100. For a reason lost to time, they wore French berets at their meetings.

In 1977, Bob Bontempo established the Executive Club. Many professionals weren't working Wednesday afternoons, and Bob brought them together for a round of golf. He'd set the teams, they'd place a small wager, and after the round everyone would repair to a restaurant for socializing and dinner. Over time the outings were reduced to once a month, with Marv Whitehead, Bill Smith, and Len Finkowski organizing the events. The group was still gathering until 2020, when Covid shut it down.

In the late 1980s Earl Gauthier and Ed Moriarty started the Pine Tree Gang. They had retired and were looking for a morning game. About a dozen men showed up at first, standing under the pines as they waited for others to arrive. They'd form teams, and everyone would wager a dollar. The Gang would go to another course for an outing each year and have an end-of-season banquet. The Pine Tree Gang still plays, now four days a week, with 12 to 20 members arriving each morning. The entry fee is \$5—enough for everyone to try to win, yet not precipitating ill will if a teammate doesn't earn his "point."

Given The Orchards' comparatively modest clubhouse and open membership policy, members of wealthy and exclusive clubs around Boston might view the Club as nothing more than an expensive municipal course with a first-rate layout. But that would be unfair to its members. At a muni, people don't serve on committees to help run the club. They don't volunteer, often anonymously, to wipe down golf carts or clean out brooks when the club is understaffed. And they don't hold fundraisers at the clubhouse for friends in need. Members of The Orchards have done these uncompensated tasks and many more because they love the Club. "It's in my heart," one remarked. Not many munis, or swanky clubs, for that matter, can boast such fealty.

Cheryl with the winner's paraphernalia. *(Margie Riley)*

Cheryl Krueger

"I was putting well that day."

"I've always enjoyed competing," Cheryl Krueger says, "and I liked to practice." Maybe that explains why she became such a good golfer. Since 2002 she has won 18 Women's Club Championships at The Orchards, and at 59, she isn't stopping.

Raised in California, Cheryl eventually moved to Delaware, where she started to play the game. She later settled in Massachusetts and met Frank Szela, who played at The Orchards. Soon she left Hickory Ridge to play in South Hadley. A self-described golf junkie, Cheryl enjoys reading everything about the game, from its history to its architects. She understands what makes a good course, and she considers The Orchards one of the best in the area. "It's difficult," Cheryl says in a respectful way. If she has been playing well at the Club, she knows her game will travel well to the other courses she plays.

She shot a 69 at The Orchards during one of the Women's Club Championships, posting a 31 on the front nine, which included a double bogey on the 1st hole. She ended her round with a 38 on the back. "I was putting well that day," she allowed. No kidding!

Titleist
2016 BMW Charity Pro-Am
Presented by SYNNEX Corporation
CHAMPION

28

Richy Werenski

"My parents have done everything to support me."

WITH THE POSSIBLE exception of Jimmy Young, Richy Werenski is the best golfer The Orchards ever produced. He had a couple of advantages most boys didn't enjoy as he was learning to play. Both his parents were excellent golfers, who helped him and his brother, Mickey, along the way. His father, Mike, was a top regional amateur and club professional, and his mother, Sue, played for the Mount Holyoke Lyons. As for the other advantage, well, he grew up in a house that was just a driver and a wedge away from The Orchards.

Like so many youngsters who play out their dreams on a golf course, Richy remembers all the hours he spent on the 18th green at The Orchards, pretending he was putting to win a major tournament, usually the Masters. He attended Heritage Academy in Hilton Head, South Carolina, then became an Academic All-ACC player at Georgia Tech, graduating in 2014. He didn't enter the professional ranks in the conventional way, however. By winning the Golf Channel's "Big Break the Palm Beaches" competition in 2015, he earned a spot in the PGA's Barbasol Championship and finished a respectable 72nd. The following year he was competing on the Web.com tour when he won his first big event, the BMW Charity Pro-Am. By 2017 he had earned his PGA tour card, and while playing in his 100th event, in 2020, he won the Barracuda Championship in Reno, Nevada.

Richy and his wife, Jordan, recently moved to Aiken, South Carolina, just across the state line from Augusta, with plenty of land on which to hunt, fish, and dirt-bike, his favorite pastimes. His parents and his brother also moved to the area. Should he qualify to play in the Masters, a lifelong dream of his, then, like the trip from his South Hadley home to the 18th green at The Orchards, he'll have just a short drive to Augusta—an advantage that served him well in the past.

Richy won the BMW Charity Pro-Am in 2016 ***(Fred Rollison)*****; Above: Richy standing behind his brother, Mickey.**

2021 CHAMPIONS

Left: The Elisabeth Skinner Invitational Trophy *(Michael Carroll)*; **Top: the author presenting this trophy to Linda Petrozzi and Lynn Oberbillig.** *(Staff of The Orchards)*; **Above: Nicole Melton, Women's Club Champion, and Kevin Reale, Men's Club Champion**

Above: Winners of the Silverwood Cup, a team event for members. Right: Bob Phelan and James Ryan, winners of the James D. Young Member-Guest Tournament *(Staff of The Orchards)*; Far right: The Jimmy Young Trophy. *(Michael Carroll)*

Celebrities Visit The Orchards

Actor Craig T. Nelson. ***(MovieStillsDB)***

NBA legend Bill Russell. ***(Getty)***

Hall of Fame pitcher Warren Spahn was in the area to help the Holyoke Millers, farm team of the California Angels. ***(Associated Press)***

SWINGING SPAHN — Baseball Hall of Fame pitcher Warren Spahn, presently the minor league pitching coach for the California Angels, swings and watches ball while playing golf at the Orchards Golf Course in South Hadley Friday. Spahn is in the area to help pitchers o[f] the Holyoke Millers, the Angels' Eastern League team. (T-T Photos Roback)

Cummington, Massachusetts, resident Secretary George Shultz often played at the Club. He claimed to have made a hole-in-one on the 5th hole, but only Secret Service men saw it. Do they count as eye-witnesses? *(Alamy)*

UMass graduate Julius Erving was certainly the tallest member of The Orchards. For five years he hosted the Jack Leaman Memorial Tournament, which was attended by professional basketball players, including Bill Russell, during the week of the Basketball Hall of Fame induction ceremony in Springfield. *(Alamy)*

"This is truly a great golf course." —George Shultz

(Michael Carroll)

Part Six

From Tree to Green

29
Trees

"You can grow trees or grass—you can't have both."
—Bob Ford, Oakmont Country Club

I think that I shall never see
A poem lovely as a tree . . .
Poems are made by fools like me,
But only God can make a tree.
—Joyce Kilmer

WHY CAN'T TREES and golf courses peacefully coexist? If golfing is meant to be an enjoyable walk through nature, why don't architects want them near their courses? And why have so many greens committees removed them since the beginning of the millennium? What felony did these innocent bystanders commit?

The answer is complicated. Golf course architects, especially those from Scotland, wanted a clean landscape, something akin to the courses they knew in their youth, with no trees interfering with play. In their seaside setting, links courses didn't need trees for beauty or aesthetics. However, golf course owners in America, especially those with parkland layouts, wanted trees, not just for their beauty, but for the definition they brought to each hole. So they planted them without remorse.

Donald Ross cautioned owners against planting too many trees. He understood they weren't good for the grass. The shade they cast over the property, the wind they blocked, and the water and nutrients they devoured for themselves, rather than for the grass, were unhealthy for a course. He wasn't against the idea of strategically locating some trees on a course, as long as they were off to the side of the rough and were spaced far enough apart so that a ball could be played from them. This made for a good recovery shot, a part of the game he valued.

Beginning in the mid-1990s, Oakmont Country Club in Pennsylvania, owner of one of America's great golf courses, began removing its trees. Not merely a few, but all of them. Incredibly, since the project was begun at night, hundreds were removed before members realized what was happening. As one can imagine, heated discussions ensued, and although no fists were thrown, some members prayed in church for their deciduous friends.

Their prayers went unanswered, as 15,000 trees were eventually removed. The club said it wanted to return the course to its appearance when Henry Fownes built it in 1903. It was

(Hans Teensma)

Top: Some of the dying red pines ***(Hans Teensma)*****. Above: More than 1,000 trees were cut down in early 2021.** ***(Michael Carroll)***

originally meant to be a links-style course without trees. Plus, they were well aware that trees can impede the growth of grass.

Shortly after The Orchards was completed, Joseph Skinner purchased 2,000 4-inch red pine saplings from a farm in New Hampshire. They were planted mostly along the perimeter of the fairways, a project that took two years to complete. But 90 years later, these pines are dying from a root fungus. (Those around the Quabbin Reservoir suffered from the same blight.) The College hadn't been thinning the clusters over the years, and their close proximity to one another made it easier for the fungus to spread. Course superintendent Dave Parson predicted they all would be dead by 2023.

Parson had been planning their removal since he arrived in 2017. His greatest concern was the risk that a tree might fall. One had already tumbled onto a golf cart out on the course, but fortunately no one was injured. Parson was also considering the health of the grass. This is especially important at The Orchards, where many holes sit on low-lying land and drainage is poor. Grass needs sunshine and air flow to help it dry out.

Although many members knew the project was imminent, they hadn't appreciated its scope until they returned to the course in early 2021. Large swaths of trees were removed, with thousands more slated to come down before the project would be complete. As at Oakmont, there was grumbling. Parson didn't need to remove so many, some members said. The thinning took away from the beauty of the course. However, given their respect for their superintendent, their voices were muted. It was only when he put an X on a hickory tree on the 18th green that the membership overruled him. They wanted the hardwoods to stand, even if they impeded course maintenance, as the one on 18 did.

The project had to be done, but to remove all the trees

on the course, as Oakmont did, wouldn't make sense. The Orchards has too many, and most are far removed from the holes. Moreover, it's an inland course in Massachusetts, where tree-lined layouts are the norm. It's best that the Club remove all dead and dying trees as well as those that impede play, and routinely thin those that remain. Otherwise, let them be. They're beautiful.

(Hans Teensma)

(Dave Fraser)

Apple Trees

The golf course got its name from the Skinner estate across the street, which was called The Orchards for the many apple trees in the back of the property. The name carried over to the course, although there weren't a lot of apple trees in 1922. There were some on the hill, which would become the 1st fairway, and a few near the driving range, but not many more.

Today there are only four or five apple trees on the course, located beside the 13th green. Members enjoy eating their fruit. The large apple tree to the right of the 4th green, which witnessed everything from Elisabeth's mashie shot to Meg Mallon's miraculous 54-foot putt, eventually died of old age. A couple of years later, a young, healthy apple was planted in its spot. Hopefully the superintendent's axe won't find it.

The 10th green (top) and the 16th green. *(Dave Fraser)*

30

Are 10 and 16 Sinking?

"No green lasts forever."

THOSE WHO RECALL playing the course in the 1960s and '70s swear that both of these greens are sinking. Their fronts are drooping toward the brook, they say, and the slopes are more severe than they remember. Today, if a ball isn't hit to at least the middle of these greens, it will roll back toward the brook. If the shot is too long, then chipping is treacherous.

Paul Jamrog, who was course superintendent from 1984 until the beginning of 1994, came back to play The Orchards in 2019. He doesn't believe they have sagged since his tenure, although older members were mentioning it in the 1980s.

The greens are cut more closely today than they were in 1922, so maybe they're just outdated. They weren't designed with fast speeds in mind. But it's hard to believe Ross would have designed greens with so much slope, regardless of the manner in which they were cut. Unfortunately, the blueprint for the 10th green (originally the 5th) doesn't provide the answer. The sectional drawing of the green is from the front, not the side. The blueprint for the 16th green (originally the 7th) doesn't include a sectional drawing; however, Walter Hatch's notations give a clue: "Flatten top of knoll to give cup space of at least 50–60 feet, *with gentle slope off in all directions*." Not every green or hole was built to the exact specifications of the blueprints, but if this one was, then clearly this green has been sagging toward the brook. Equally compelling is that both greens sit on wetlands, so some shifting can be expected over time.

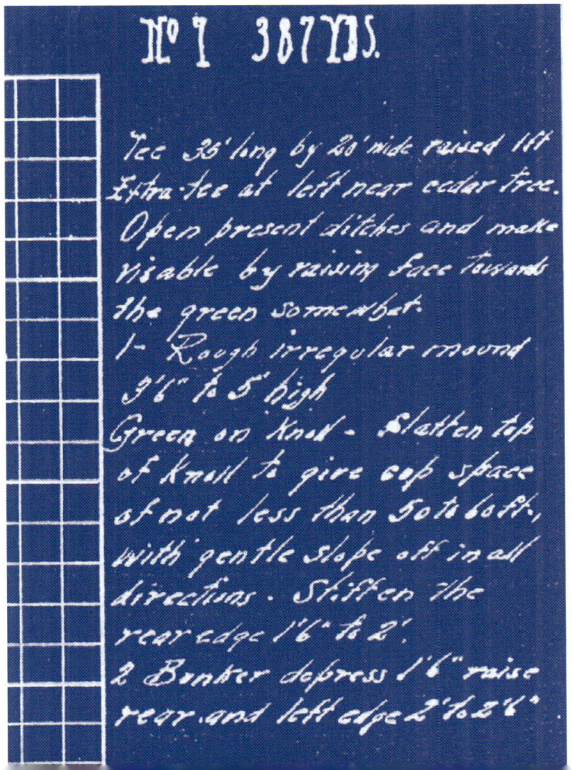

It's a testament to the quality of Ross's construction that most of the greens at The Orchards have survived as long as they have. But no green lasts forever. Maybe it's time to do something with these two.

(Michael Carroll)

Part Seven
Looking Back, Looking Ahead

31

Remembering Donald Ross

"Design on land, not on paper."

DONALD ROSS VISITED the Holyoke/South Hadley area many times. He was likely on site at The Orchards in 1921, the year he was remodeling Mt. Tom in Holyoke, and he returned to South Hadley in 1927 to add nine holes. His only child, Lillian, attended Mount Holyoke College from 1928 to 1932, and he frequently came up from Pinehurst to see her. He would return in 1936 for her wedding; the reception was held at the Mt. Tom clubhouse. Despite the many trips Ross made to the area and the opportunities he had to play The Orchards, there's no record he ever did.

Lillian Ross, member of the Class of 1932. ***(WGBY)***

Ross had a remarkable career, building or remodeling more than 400 courses. When he was absent, two associates did quality work for the 30 percent of the courses he probably never saw, and they helped grow his business to a size that would otherwise have been unattainable.

However, if an architect is to put his name on a blueprint, it isn't enough for him to review sketches from afar, as Ross often did. He needs to walk the property to feel its contours, assess the soil, see the obstacles, and imagine the possibilities if he is to do his best work. When his career came to an end, Ross regretted that he had designed so many courses, since he wasn't on-site to see them all.

Golf course architecture has evolved in America since Ross left the scene, but very few architects are as revered as he is. The artistry of his work, the design of his greens, and the playability of his courses for golfers of all abilities are hallmarks that endure.

Donald Ross in Pinehurst, N.C. ***(Tufts Archives)***

Massachusetts Golf Courses Designed by Donald Ross

Ross wasn't confirmed to have been on-site for over half the golf courses he designed in the state.

COURSE	YEAR BUILT	CONFIRMED ON SITE
Bass River Golf Course	1914	No
Belmont Country Club	1918	Yes
Brae Burn Country Club	1912	Yes
Charles River	1921	Yes
Cohasse Country Club	1916	No
Cohasset Golf Club	1922	Yes
Commonwealth G.C.	1921	No
Concord Country Club	1915	Yes
C.C. of New Bedford	1924	No
C.C. of Pittsfield	1921	No
Ellinwood C.C.	1920	No
Essex County Club	1909	Yes
Franklin Park G.C.	1922	No
George Wright G.C.	1938	Yes
Greenock Country Club	1927	No
Hyannisport Club	1936	No
Island Country Club	1913	No
Kernwood Country Club	1914	Yes
Longmeadow C. C.	1921	Yes
Ludlow Country Club	1920	No
Merrimack Valley G.C.	1906	No
Nantucket Golf Links	1917	No
North Andover C.C.	1920	No
Oak Hill Country Club	1921	Yes
Oakley Country Club	1900	Yes
Oyster Harbors G.C.	1927	Yes
Petersham C.C.	1922	No

COURSE	YEAR BUILT	CONFIRMED ON SITE
Plymouth C. C.	1929	Yes
Pocasset Golf Club	1916	No
Ponkapoag G.C.	1931	No
Salem Country Club	1925	Yes
Sandy Burr	1925	Yes
Springfield C.C.	1924	No
Tatnuck Country Club	1930	No
Tedesco Country Club	1937	No
Tekoa Country Club	1923	No
The Orchards	1922	No
The Orchards	1927	Yes
Toytown Tavern Club	1924	Yes
Vesper Country Club	1919	No
Wachusett C.C.	1911	No
Waltham C.C.	1921	No
Wellesley C.C.	1911	No
Weston G.C.	1916	Yes
Weston G.C.	1923	No
Whaling City G.C.	1920	No
Whitinsville G.C.	1925	No
Wianno Golf Club	1913	No
Winchester C.C.	1903	Yes
Winchester C.C.	1928	No
Woodland G.C.	1928	No
Worcester C.C.	1913	Yes
Wyckoff Park G.C.	1923	Yes

From Discovering Donald Ross by *Bradley Klein*

32

Looking Ahead

"Don't do a thing to the Ross layout, just take care of it."

How will history record future events at The Orchards? It's impossible to see too far ahead with clarity. Since 1922 our lives, our work, and our pastimes have changed dramatically. When the course was built, baseball, boxing, and horse racing were America's favorite sports. Two of those sports are barely surviving today. Golf's popularity in America vacillated over those years. The economic booms in the 1920s and the final decades of the 20th century ushered in a record number of courses. But the Depression slowed golf course development in the 1930s, and the stock market crashes in 2001 and 2008 put a firm brake on its growth. Between 2003 and 2018, more than 1,200 courses closed, as 6.8 million fewer Americans were playing the game. There were too many golf courses and too few players.

(Hans Teensma)

So what about The Orchards? How healthy will it be in the decades ahead? Because of its pedigree and the quality of its layout, golfers will always want to play the course. After Taconic, in Williamstown, it is arguably the best course in western Massachusetts. However, golfers will join the Club only if the cost of membership is right and the course is in good condition. Otherwise, they'll go elsewhere.

Mount Holyoke College will determine both outcomes when the 25-year lease it entered into with Palmer runs out at the end of 2024. The rent it charges the next lessee must be reduced to give the manager a chance to make a profit. Otherwise, it won't have an incentive to invest in the property, and the course will suffer. Also, the College must recognize that The Orchards won't draw members from beyond western Massachusetts, so the money it expects to receive should reflect that reality.

(Michael Carroll)

The Orchards has seen it all over the past 100 years—from a tristate champion, to a husband and wife team who dedicated 38 years of service to the Club, to an era when golf carts replaced caddies, to an automated irrigation system, two USGA championships, and many successful Lyons teams. For the Club to regain the enviable position it once enjoyed, with a list of people waiting to join, it should follow the prescription from the past: Don't do a thing to the Donald Ross layout it has been blessed to play, just take care of it.

When Joseph Skinner asked Donald Ross to design The Orchards in 1921, he certainly did it for Elisabeth. Yet in the end, Elisabeth was right when she explained his motivation: "Father wanted the townspeople to have a nice place to play." And that they do.

Why?

Companies like to rebrand things, as Nike did when it changed its name from Blue Ribbon Sports. Other times they do it to kick-start a languishing product, so "New and Improved" is often proclaimed. But The Orchards wasn't languishing in 1999; its membership ranks were full, and its name didn't need more luster. So why did the Palmer Group drop "The" from its name to identify it as Orchards?

Did it believe a new name would connote improvement, to perhaps attract golfers from Boston? Was it to distinguish the course from other golf courses of the same name? Yes, there are others, but the course in South Hadley is at least 70 years older than they are, and, ahem, it's a Donald Ross design.

With the Palmer lease expiring at the end of 2024, Club members should start a movement to bring back the "The"!

(Michael Carroll)

View of the Summit House atop Mount Holyoke. *(Michael Carroll)*

(Michael Carroll)

Bibliography

Fay, Michael J. *Golf as It Was Meant to Be Played.* New York: Rizzoli International, Universe Publishing, 2000.

Kilborne, Sarah S. *American Phoenix*. New York: Free Press, 2012.

Klein, Bradley S. *Rough Meditations*. Chelsea, MI: Sleeping Bear Press, 1997.

——*Discovering Donald Ross*. Duck Pond Press, 2011.

Ross, Donald J. *Golf Has Never Failed Me*. Chelsea, MI: Sleeping Bear Press, 1995.

Sheehan, Laurence, ed. *A Commonwealth of Golfers*. Norton, MA: Massachusetts Golf Association, 2002.

Thibodeau, Kate Navarra. *Holyoke: The Skinner Family and Wistariahurst*. Charleston, SC: Arcadia Publishing, 2005.

USGA. *The 2004 U.S. Women's Open: Meg-nificent*. 59 minutes, 2020.

WGBY. *From Tee to Green: The History of The Orchards*. 35 minutes, 2004.

UNPUBLISHED MATERIAL

"Conversations with Minnie, The Story of Jim and Minnie Young and The Orchards." Mount Holyoke College Archives, memoir. Minnie Young with Elva Zajac, June 1993.

"History of The Orchards: The Early Years." Interviews, Dr. Richard Maher, circa 1996.

"The Orchards and Jimmie." Mount Holyoke College Archives, memoir, Minnie Young with Elva Zajac, March 1997.

(Michael Carroll)

W
E

Appendix

Men's Club Champions

1942	Ray Roberts	1992	Peter Gordon
1945	Ray Roberts	1993	Peter Gordon
1948	Ray Roberts	1994	Alistair Catto
1949	Ray Roberts	1995	Steve Bys
1956	Ray Roberts	1996	Steve Bys
1959	Ray Roberts	1997	Jack Bresnahan Jr.
1967	Ray Roberts	1998	Don Dastoli
1969	Ray Roberts	1999	Brian Crawford
1970	Ed Pokora	2000	Keith Orlen
1971	Peter Bain	2001	Jay Donovan
1972	Ray Magdalenski	2002	Alistair Catto
1973	Jack Bresnahan Jr.	2003	Andy Dastoli
1974	Steve Kelly	2004	Jay Donovan
1975	Peter Bain	2005	Jay Donovan
1976	Peter Bain	2006	Alistair Catto
1977	Jack Bresnahan Jr.	2007	Alistair Catto
1978	Glenn Dunphy	2008	Aidan Brownlie
1979	Ed Pokora	2009	Jim Hosey
1980	Jack Bresnahan Jr.	2010	Scott Rainaud
1981	Hermas Fleury	2011	Marc Lowell
1982	Jack Bresnahan Jr.	2012	Ron Laverdiere
1983	Bill Cotti	2013	Sean Gaudette
1984	Steve Kelly	2014	Sean Gaudette
1985	Steve Kelly	2015	Andy Dastoli
1986	Steve Kelly	2016	Matt Lipinski
1987	Alistair Catto	2017	James Patterson
1988	Alistair Catto	2018	James Patterson
1989	Alistair Catto	2019	Andrew Rogers
1990	Dean Godek	2020	Cody Miller
1991	Dean Godek	2021	Kevin Reale

Women's Club Champions

1963	Ada Lawler	1993	Bonnie Catto
1964	Ceil Harnisch	1994	Bonnie Catto
1965	Betty Washburn	1995	Bonnie Catto
1966	Ceil Harnisch	1996	Marti Cain
1967	Shirley Livi	1997	Bonnie Catto
1968	Shirley Livi	1998	Bonnie Catto
1969	Ruth Borgatti	1999	Cheryl Krueger
1970	Ruth Borgatti	2000	Bonnie Catto
1971	Norma Nobbs	2001	Laura Orlen
1972	Yvette Swol	2002	Cheryl Krueger
1973	Shirley Livi	2003	Bonnie Catto
1974	Lillian Johnson	2004	Cheryl Krueger
1975	Yvette Swol	2005	Cheryl Krueger
1976	Roz Nozik	2006	Cheryl Krueger
1977	Anita Wilson	2007	Cheryl Krueger
1978	Dorothy Frey	2008	Cheryl Krueger
1979	Joann Smith	2009	Cheryl Krueger
1980	Ilyne Paul	2010	Cheryl Krueger
1981	Sue Marion	2011	Cheryl Krueger
1982	Sue Marion	2012	Cheryl Krueger
1983	Dorene Janes	2013	Cheryl Krueger
1984	Sue Marion	2014	Cheryl Krueger
1985	Lillian Johnson	2015	Cheryl Krueger
1986	Dorothy Frey	2016	Kimberlee Green
1987	Sue Werenski	2017	Cheryl Krueger
1988	Sue Werenski	2018	Cheryl Krueger
1989	Bonnie Catto	2019	Cheryl Krueger
1990	Bonnie Catto	2020	Cheryl Krueger
1991	Shawn Chalmers	2021	Nicole Melton
1992	Bonnie Catto		

James D. Young Member–Guest Winners

1959	Walt Haglund and Joe Olko
1960	Gay Knapp and Frank Comfort
1961	Ray Roberts and Ed Costa
1962	Bernie Rubin and Ed Costa
1963	Gardner Thompson and George Abdow
1964	Al Doyle and Mike Higgins
1965	Ken Burgess and Joe Feicha
1966	Gardner Thompson and George Abdow
1967	Ray Magdalenski and Jon Hunt
1968	Gardner Thompson and George Abdow
1969	Mitch Alexander and Joe Mullarkey
1970	Ray Magdalenski and Jon Hunt
1971	Steve Kelly and Ed Bilik
1972	George Orlen and Ron Collins
1973	Walt Garbacik and Wally Garbacik
1974	Keith Quenneville and Jack Dunn
1975	Tom Szwedzinski and Kurt Wajda
1976	Jack Bresnahan Jr. and Gene Quenneville
1977	Peter Bain and Ed Garbacik
1978	Ed Garbacik and Peter Bain
1979	Bill Dupont and Jon Stavros
1980	Vern Mongeau and Don Dastoli
1981	Stan O'Connell and Tom Morrison
1982	John Griffin and Tim Collins
1983	Bob McGee and Ed Quigley Jr.
1984	Tom Skowron and Doug Harper
1985	Bernie Crawford and Bill Skiba
1986	Dean Godek and Brad Klinkowski
1987	Alistair Catto and Gary Burt
1988	Dave Oldershaw and Chris Burke
1989	Jack Bresnahan Jr. and Flynt Lincoln
1990	Rick Durocher and Steve Elkins
1991	Dean Godek and Greg Orili
1992	Chris Lapinski and Steve Lavoie
1993	Tom Bergeron and Gary Burt
1994	Tom Bergeron and Gary Burt
1995	Ralph Strolis and Dennis Booska
1996	Bill House and Kim Michael Mertes
1997	Dick Barber and Tom Bergeron
1998	Mike Ryan and James Ryan
1999	Fan Gaudette and Mike Majka
2000	Peter Gordon and Chris Burke
2001	Fan Gaudette and Mike Majka
2002	Greg Folsom and Chris Ferriter
2003	Dave Oldershaw and Chris Burke
2004	Keith Orlen and Greg Folsom
2005	Mike Burke and Chris Ferriter
2004	Keith Orlen and Greg Folsom
2005	Mike Burke and Chris Ferriter
2006	Michael Wiernasz and Rob Tedoldi
2007	James Ryan and Brian Foley
2008	Chris Ferriter and Chris Burke
2009	Mark Manca and Geoff Tobia
2010	Joe Premont and Jim Mucchino
2011	Scott Aye and Kevin Kinne
2012	Ivan Marshal and Eric Peterson
2013	Doug Perrin and Jon Shea
2014	Jim Hosey and Bobby Linn
2015	Andy Dastoli and Steve Diemesevich
2016	Tyler Beaudry and Dave Laporte
2017	Eric Jewett and Jamie Griffiths
2018	William Ingham and Matt Lapinski
2019	Bob Phelan and James Ryan
2020	not contested
2021	Bob Phelan and James Ryan

Orchards Women's Invitational Winners

1983	Roberta Bolduc and Ann Southworth
1984	Susan McLellan and Karen Laverdiere
1985	Roberta Bolduc and Ann Southworth
1986	Joyce Martin and Pam Zanetto
1987	Joyce Martin and Pam Zanetto
1988	Joyce Martin and Pam Zanetto
1989	Joyce Martin and Pam Zanetto
1990	Sue Wilson and Renee Swirsky
1991	Joyce Martin and Pam Zanetto
1992	Chris Caney and Deb Patten
1993	Joyce Martin and Betsy Drambour
1994	Joyce Martin and Betsy Drambour
1995	Pam Zanetto and Deb Bloom
1996	Marti Cain and Bonnie Catto
1997	Marti Cain and Bonnie Catto
1998	Chris Caney and Karen Podgorski
1999	Chris Caney and Karen Podgorski
2000	Deb Bloom and Pam Zanetto
2001	Deb Bloom and Pam Zanetto
2002	Deb Patten and Lynn Oberbillig
2003	Betty Dubois and Mary Harris
2004	Deb Bloom and Pam Zanetto
2005	Lyn Modzelesky and Sue Nilsen
2006	Deb Bloom and Pam Zanetto
2007	Deb McCulloch and Tara Zidonic
2008	Lyne Kendall and Irene Lee
2009	Deb McCulloch and Tara Zidoni
2010	Cathy Sessions and Marjorie Funk
2011	Patricia Mayne and Karen Feldman
2012	Patricia Mayne and Karen Feldman
2013	Cathy Sessions and Vicki Staebler

Elisabeth Skinner Invitational Winners

2015	Kathi Sorey and Ellen Mordas
2016	Nora Patton and Cathy Sessions
2017	Linda Petrozzi and Lynn Oberbillig
2018	Cheryl Krueger and Cathy Sessions
2019	not contested
2020	not contested
2021	Lynn Oberbillig and Linda Petrozzi

Head Golf Professionals Through 2021

Jimmy Young
Dan Webster
Bob Bontempo
Ed Twohig, Jr.
Bob McHugh
Jim Stickles
Greg Lauzier
Jonathan Banas
Keith Cunningham

Significant Events Held at The Orchards

AIAW

1973 National Collegiate Tournament
1979 Eastern Collegiate Tournament
1980 Eastern Collegiate Tournament

Interscholastic

1975 Eastern Interscholastic Tournament
1976 Eastern Interscholastic Tournament

NCAA

1993 Women's Division II and III National Championship
2002 Women's Division III National Championship

USGA

1987 U.S. Girls' Junior Championship
2003 U.S. Women's Open Qualifer
2003 U.S. Senior Amateur Qualifier
2004 U.S. Women's Open
2007 U.S. Amateur Qualifier
2012 U.S. Amateur Qualifier
2015 U.S. Mid-Amateur Qualifier
2016 U.S. Amateur Qualifier
2019 U.S. Mid-Amateur Qualifier

Women's Golf Association of Massachusetts

1991 Edith Noblit Baker Trophy
1995 Women's Amateur Championship
2013 Junior Tri-State Matches
2017 Eleanor I. Labonte Tournament

Massachusetts Golf Association

1990 Mass Four Ball Championship
1994 Mass Junior Amateur Championship
2001 Mass Amateur Championship
2010 Mass Senior Four Ball Championship
2017 Mass Junior Amateur Championship
2021 Mass Girls Junior Amateur Championship
2022 Mass Women's Amateur Championship

PGA

1966 Connecticut Assistants Championship
1968 Connecticut Championship
1968 Connecticut Senior Championship
2009 Connecticut Walter Lowell
2012 Connecticut Walter Lowell
2014 Connecticut Championship
2017 Connecticut Pro-Junior Invitational
2022 Connecticut Match Play Championship

Western Mass Open

2019, 2020, 2021

Endicott Cup

2000

(Dave Fraser)

Acknowledgments

This book could not have been completed without the generous help of many individuals. Everyone was supportive of my mission and eager to assist me. The information, recommendations, photographs, and other material they shared proved invaluable. I am especially indebted to Mary Chaffee, who wrote so beautifully of her grandparents, Jimmy and Minnie Young.

My sincere thanks to John Adams, Bob Bontempo, Susan Bushey-Manning, Bonnie Catto, Carl Chaffee, Eileen Crosby of the Holyoke Public Library, Bill Dupont, Shawn Durocher, Joe Ferrantino, Leslie Fields of Mount Holyoke College, Tom Feitel, Len Finkowski, Dave Fraser, Sally Hart, Dorene Janes, Paul Jamrog, Sarah Kilborne, Bradley Klein, Cheryl Krueger, Penni Martorell of Wistariahurst Museum, Audrey Moriarty of Tufts Archives, Chris Morris, Laurie Priest, Mike and Margie Riley, the staff of the United States Golf Association, Margaret Selig, Chris Tallman, Anne Marie Tobin, Dick Towne, Barry Waite, Fred Waterman, Bonita Wilson of Callaway Golf, Tom Wylie, Bill Young, and Jason Young.